Jane,

May you be held
by these words,

Michelle

Cry of the Nightbird:
Writers Against Domestic Violence

Edited by

Michelle Wing
Ann Hutchinson
Kate Farrell

Michelle Wing
Oct. 2014

WolfSinger Publications   Security, Colorado

Cover art copyright © 2014 by Sonja Bauer
Interior photos copyright – Carrie Nassif
Illustrations in *In the Darkest Times* copyright - Megan Ingrassia

ISBN: 978-1-936099-67-2
Printed and bound in the United States of America

Dedication

To the Reader

By reading and thoughtfully considering the contributions of the writers featured in these pages, you join the ranks of those who recognize the devastating effects of domestic violence. More importantly, you help to begin a much needed healing in our community where one in four families are affected. The mission of YWCA is to end domestic violence in Sonoma County through awareness, education, and empowerment.

It is with immense gratitude to Michelle Wing, author, poet, angel, and creator of the Changing Hurt to Hope Writers' Series that we at YWCA Sonoma County honor Michelle for her work that has inspired the creation of this volume.

Madeleine Keegan O'Connell
Chief Executive Officer
YWCA Sonoma County

Gifts
Michelle Wing

You come to me as electronic messages,
envelopes filled with lamentation
coursing through the air in search
      of a place to touch ground.

Stories of grief, of loss, of families
ripped apart, torn limb from limb, mothers bruised,
children terrified, fathers imprisoned by alcohol,
      legacies of pain.

And yet each missive arrives bundled
in courage, wrapped up with hope,
looking towards a future without
      hiding or fear.

One by one, I receive these offerings,
open my hands to hold them,
pull them in close to my chest,
      and breathe in thanks.

You are brave–I honor you.
You are resilient–I am humbled by you.
You are powerful–I draw strength from you.
      Each one of you is a gift.

Dedicated to all the contributors to
Changing Hurt to Hope: Writers Speak Out
Against Domestic Violence

Foreword

In *Cry of the Nightbird: Writers Against Domestic Violence*, thirty-eight writers speak out in prose and poems of a hidden tragedy: violence in homes, living in fear, and forced silence. Authors from every walk of life and every aspect of this difficult issue raise their voices as one to end this silence, to bring freedom and release for themselves and for others. These words will inform and inspire readers: give them eyes to see, a way to express, and motivation to act.

Domestic violence knows no borders and does not exempt anyone based on class, color, gender, or sexual orientation. Every twenty-four minutes, someone is a victim of physical violence, rape, or stalking by an intimate partner in the United States: twelve million women and men each year, or three in ten women and one in ten men. But it is not just these victims who are affected; the entire community pays a price. This book presents the stories behind the numbers, brings us inside frightening moments of denial, crisis, and escape through the media of literary and visual arts.

Cry of the Nightbird: Writers Against Domestic Violence selects the best of short fiction, personal narrative, poetry, and art from YWCA Sonoma County's "Changing Hurt to Hope: Writers Speak out Against Domestic Violence" reading series, now in its fifth year. In answer to an open call sent out to the community first in 2010, writers responded with their works, then gathered to read them aloud during October's Domestic Violence Awareness Month in several different cities throughout Sonoma County.

Michelle Wing, Ann Hutchinson, Kate Farrell
Editors

Introduction

Sonoma County can be a wonderful place to live. It is a thriving, beautiful, wine country with unique natural resources, rich cultural diversity, and a robust entrepreneurial community. And yet, these assets cannot protect us from one of the most persistently underreported crimes—domestic violence. In Sonoma County, the YWCA Crisis Hotline alone receives more than three thousand calls annually. We know that domestic violence is one of the leading health and wellness risks for Sonoma County women and children.

Domestic violence has been called the silent tragedy, but for the victims it is anything but silent. My heart sinks when I read the headlines of yet another tragedy or when I hear of a family torn apart by abuse at the hands of someone who was in a position of trust.

Domestic violence affects all groups of people across all ethnicities, income levels, genders, sexual orientations, and social backgrounds. Sadly, the injured often suffer in silence because of the shame, fear, and humiliation that many victims feel. The wounded often believe that there is no place for them to go, a fear that is reinforced by the perpetrator. However, this is not the case here in Sonoma County. We are fortunate to have agencies like the YWCA Sonoma County always ready to provide services for victims.

As a Sonoma County Supervisor committed to public safety, I am proud to say I was part of the team, along with our District Attorney and partners, that funded and launched the Family Justice Center, a multi-disciplinary group of committed professionals, including the YWCA, who work together under one roof to provide coordinated services to victims of family violence. My vision is simple: to help family violence victims live free from violence and abuse.

I want to thank the committed advocates from the public sector, the private sector, and our community-based organizations who contribute both time and treasure to support victims of physical violence, rape, elder abuse, and stalking. Together we are making progress, although we cannot ignore that there is still more to do to raise awareness and put an end to the violence.

Cry of the Nightbird: Writers Against Domestic Violence raises our understanding to a higher level. The authors connect difficult topics to real life situations through short fiction, personal narrative, poetry, and art. I can't think of a more fitting platform for an exploration of this important and personal topic that affects our entire community.

Shirlee Zane
Sonoma County Supervisor

TABLE OF CONTENTS

NIGHT

DAWN

NOON

TWILIGHT

Night

"The oak fought the wind and was broken,
the willow bent when it must and survived."

—Robert Jordan, *The Fires of Heaven*

Carrying On
Carrie Nassif

We were hiding together in the dirt-crusted cellar,
    Death, the girl, and I
when he asked me what kind of world it was I lived in
and opened a glowing orange portal –
    a gaping square that started waist-high
to show me his.
He was just a small boy in sepia-tones handing out pills
so wide-eyed, I clambered in
        my knees awkwardly bent up to cross into the threshold
        he'd opened
        thigh-high.
There his eyes flashed black-light backlit
        all opposite and wrong
and I kissed his gleaming cheek anyhow –
drawing away with a shock:
        gritty lips,
        the smell of dark moist earth.
Numb, I silently slipped back over the highlightered outline
        of his arbitrary door
        from before
and he
he was sucked away by the howling storm
        of my leaving.
Turning my back
I hunkered down again in the cellar
        huddled over
        to cover
        the other
her baby-fat-toddler-body cradled in my arms
        till it was safe again
        at the siren's end
when we tromped to the front yard
        struggling with her limp sweltering weight clasping me grimly
        tall cold backyard grass dampening my bare legs
and surveyed the damage
we'd have to pretend wasn't there.

The Hardest Part

Erin Treanor

I remember the first time it happened. Well, actually he had punched me before, once. And I was dumb enough to think that didn't mean anything. It was a long time before anything happened again. In fact I had completely forgotten about it. I felt like it didn't count. How weird is that?

The next time it happened was just a little worse. We were screaming at each other over the usual things: bills, the dishes, laundry. And I saw his face change, eyes darken. Turns out it's really true, that happens.

I was usually on the defense in arguments: Always, I'm so sorry, it won't happen again, we can change this, fix that. That night I stood my ground. I felt strong, smart. I looked him right in the eye, and was confident that no one would speak to me that way.

He took me by the face and threw me onto a fan that was running on the floor. It was one of those old rusty, shitty ones. Not sure why that sticks in my head, but it does. Anyway, one of the blades sliced into my leg. I don't even remember much pain. I mean it hurt, yes, but that's not what I remember. I remember the silence, ear-splitting, piercing silence. It was like everything just got still. I think we were both in a little bit of shock. It wasn't like the first punch that was an "accident," a quick lash out that he was sorry for, of course.

This was a clear decision. I saw it happen as his eyes darkened. I knew now that he knew what he was doing. He didn't lose his temper. He chose right then to hurt me. And as deafening as that silence was, everything was also incredibly loud! And crisp! Each little sound was so sharp. I remember a car going by on the street. A meow from a cat outside. I wasn't even breathing hard. Funny. It really is funny how absolutely calm I felt right then.

Then it was time to deal with what happened. I became very aware of just how loud the fan was. The grinding of the gears was so loud. Then I focused on the part stuck in me. I noticed I couldn't get up. I tried a couple times.

He didn't move.

I tried to pull the blade out. It was stuck.

He didn't move.

It started to hurt more. I felt around the back of my leg. It felt wet. I looked at my hand and saw blood.

He didn't move.

I had to get up. It sounds stupid, but all I could think about was not getting blood on the carpet! Dumb! All I could think was either I was moving out and wanted to get my deposit back, or I would come home every day and be reminded by the blood on the carpet at the foot of our bed. I looked at him and he looked back at me.

He didn't move.

You know, the hardest part wasn't the pain in my leg. It wasn't even the pain in my heart. It wasn't the sadness I felt because this was where I was in my life. The hardest part was when I looked up at him and said, "Pull this out for me please."

He bent over and got it. I asked, "Help me up?" He did, gently.

"I need to get to the bathroom and clean it, see if this is bad." I realized I couldn't put weight on that side, so I asked, "Get me into the bathroom?" Of course I still couldn't see it; I couldn't turn that way. Being short didn't help me see much in our apartment mirror. I had to ask, "Look at it. Is it bad? Can I just clean it or do I need a doctor?"

He knelt behind me and said, "I can't see much through the hole in your pants. I need to take these off to see it."

I stood there, cold. Shut down. Focused. While he pulled my pants down, knelt behind me, and cleaned and dressed my leg. I stood there, knowing what my life would be. I knew it then.

But I still say, the hardest part wasn't the fight. The hardest part wasn't the pain, the emotion or the fall. And it wasn't even the fear that I felt then and that would become very familiar. No, the hardest part was when I realized I needed to ask for help from the only person in the room. I needed to ask for help from him.

And while that was the hardest part, the worst part was when I accepted it.

The Cage
Leonore Wilson

They were on the opposite side of the highway, he in his red Camaro throwing her out like garbage. I watched her trip on her heels,

her little black bag catch in the door's handle. He was pounding her back and shoving her, it was as if her feet were caught in stirrups,

and a stallion was bucking off its rider, but its rider was helpless, it kept staying on, it couldn't get off, all the contraptions that held the rider

to the mount resisted freedom. Then she fell to the ground. I could see she tried not to fall too clumsy, as if not to break her nails or ruin her make-up.

I shouted at her as she ran across the highway, the cars honking as if she was a dog in traffic that broke its leash. I called for her

and she saw me, I called for her with the door open, and she came in so matter of factly. I saw her beauty then, her youth. She was a young Filipina

girl with the hard purple lipstick, and the black straight hair the color of ink. She had the tight jeans, sheer blouse, little breasts uplifted in lace.

I saw his rage come at me across the highway. I saw she and I were prey. We were one. We were two animals hunted. This was the city

that keeps animals in cages that mimic Africa. Big animals that circle their cells, sit in their own excrement and do tricks.

Elephants that put their big feet on painted pails and wave their back legs while the whole audience applauds. Exotic butterflies trapped in a room,

the glaze of a garden. Camels numbed to macadam and whips. He followed us as we raced through the city, honking and shouting

and rumbling his engine like a gun. Every stoplight he got out of his car, he pounded my doors with his fists, pounded the windows

as if an animal at a drive through zoo, and he could crush us, get in. But I wouldn't let him. I talked to her, I wanted to know

what I was dealing with, she said I was dealing with cocaine, I was dealing with a man in a cage. I didn't know if he was

in a cage or she was in a cage. We talked about being in cages, about how somebody had to break the cage and get out,

somebody had to change. She didn't want her father to know. She wanted me to drive her to her aunt's. I was driving a whole city,

a desert. I was weaving in and out of lanes. I was telling my entire life history as if I could save her, get her back in school, get her away from the man with cocaine.

I stopped a truckful of men on lunch break, said there was a crazy man following us. I said follow me to the police station. I could see the crazy man eying us

two stoplights back. We drove with the men out on lunch in front. They watched us go inside. The girl and I sat in the police station,

she wanted to leave, said she had a doctor's appointment, needed an exam. I asked her if she was pregnant. When she said no, I didn't believe her.

She filed a police report against him, said she did it to please me. No one wanted to take her home, the police had seen it before.

I drove her to her aunt's. No one was following. I watched her walk up to the house, chat briefly and wave. I could tell that girl wasn't truthful, she had a cockiness,

the way she talked, and moved her hips. I remember her telling me how he beat her, that one day she'd get away. I looked at the houses, beautiful and big,

I thought how some people live in houses, and in every house there is a cage.

Cinderella Tale

Meta Strauss

Brenda's Story

Brenda looked herself over in the mirror, wanting to be sure the forty-odd stitches in her head were covered by her blond hair and the colorful silk headband. After a few adjustments, she was pleased with her looks. The former beauty queen still had it!

The emergency room doctors had questioned her thoroughly about the lacerations and bruises. She was pretty sure they believed her explanation. Steve was there and acted the concerned and loving husband.

She should have known better than trying to get away from him again. She went to a divorce attorney and Steve found out, sending him into a rage. This time he had thrown her across the patio, hitting her head on a metal table. That was a week ago. Since then, she had made excuses to friends and family while hiding in her bedroom to let the injury heal.

Grabbing her handbag, Brenda checked one more time to be sure no one would question the scarf camouflage. She would meet Steve at their daughter's private school where they, as co-PTA presidents, would conduct the monthly meeting of parents and teachers.

Living around a time bomb for the past twenty-three years had created her "dual personality." Inside lived the frightened girl Steve rescued from her poor, small town family. Outside was the well-known wife of a leading defense attorney, a socially involved leader living in a big, beautiful home, wearing designer clothes.

Their teenage daughter, Marcy, was the love of her life. Steve reminded Brenda often that if she even looked like she was plotting to leave, he'd make sure she'd never see Marcy again.

As she parked her car in the school's parking lot, she saw her best friend waving to her across the line of SUVs and minivans. She knew she'd get another lecture about how dangerous Steve had become. It was difficult for anyone else to understand how it was easier to stay with Steve, keep up the charade, follow his demands, and accept the occasional beating, than it was to take another chance to break free. This was her life. She'd married him and she'd have to try harder to make him happy.

Nancy's Story

Nancy knew the minute she saw her across the parking lot at their children's school that Steve had been at it again. Brenda had a snazzy scarf wrapped skillfully around her head. It didn't fool her. They had been friends for years, served on their suburban city council together and Nancy knew all her stories.

They greeted each other on the walkway entrance to the PTA meeting room, and Nancy pulled Brenda aside. She could see the tell-tale bruise marks hidden by makeup.

"Okay, when did this happen? How many stitches do you have?" Nancy asked.

Brenda glanced around cautiously and whispered. "Forty, but he didn't mean to hurt me. He found out about my trip to the lawyer, lost his temper, and threw me into the metal patio furniture."

"Good God! Surely I can talk some sense into your pretty little head this time. Brenda, he is dangerous," scolded Nancy. Steve scared her to death. The rich scumbag's violent outbursts seemed to get worse with time. She thought, *What can I do to intervene in this situation? I feel powerless, but something has to be done, and soon. If Lou ever did to me, even once, what Steve has done to her many times, I'd be gone!*

When they arrived at the meeting, every man in the room turned to look at Brenda. Not only was she strikingly gorgeous, but her personality was a radiant force. Nancy had to bite her lips when she saw Steve lean over and kiss Brenda on the cheek. The perfect husband! What a joke. She wanted to scream out the truth to the entire, assembled parents' organization. The handsome, successful, and certifiably crazy Steve! She would do something next week. She knew there were agencies that could help.

Matt's Story

That Saturday night at seven o'clock, Matt, Marcy's boyfriend, rang her doorbell. He was decked out in his rented tux and his sweaty palms held the corsage he'd ordered from the florist. He wanted this night to be the most special Marcy had ever had. Strange. There was no answer.

He knocked and rang the bell repeatedly. They had to be at home, because all the cars were in the carport. The lights were on, and he could hear music playing. He walked around the house and peeked inside. Nothing! Finally, Matt returned to his car and called Marcy's number. Again, nothing!

Ten minutes passed. Matt's stomach churned as he called his parents. "Mom, something is wrong."

Marcy acted like she lived in a Cinderella Fairy Tale, but he knew better. She denied the violence between her parents, but he had seen her mom's bruises. He sensed her relationship with her dad was odd. When he questioned her about it, she said her dad had some problems and then dismissed any further conversation. He was waiting anxiously for the day Marcy would leave for college and get away.

Matt's parents arrived, knocking on doors and peering in windows. Then they called the police. Within the hour the beautiful prom evening turned upside down into the most horrible of Matt's eighteen years. Marcy's house was surrounded by police cars, two ambulances, and the Coroner's official vehicle.

Matt would never again see Marcy alive. She would not be able to fulfill her dreams. Brenda would never be beaten again. Steve would never lose his temper again. Nancy wouldn't be able to help Brenda. It was too late.

Steve shot Brenda once in the back of her head. She was found in their bedroom. He shot Marcy three times as she had tried to get away from him in the hallway. He then shot himself through the mouth and fell next to Brenda. The prom was cancelled.

How Far Have We Fallen?
Ed Thompson

What haunts me most
about this event upon the bridge
is not the arcing toss across the railing
or the impact on the concrete bosom of the ocean.
It's the fall itself,
which in my mind twists and turns
without an ending.
We hope that one so small could find delight
in being flung so long
as flight before had always ended
in the cradled arms of father;
or wish, at least, that receding bridge
and world gone topsy-turvy
distracted her from the howling wind
that would not allow for breathing.
Perhaps, a straw I know,
she could not tell which was sky
and which was water and thought
she might be falling toward the heavens.
We can hope but must suspect
that even three year olds must know
that falls will have their endings.

And then, he followed after,
as any man would have to
unless he were a demon.
Was he?
I think he might have been a man;
and though I cannot comprehend his actions,
he must have had his reasons:
She could not grow up and know
that father murdered mother;
for if she did not see the deed,
she must have heard the shotgun blast
shattered by the stillness.
Or he thought—
could he have thought at all?—

that evil only would have issued from his loins,
and he wished to rid the world
of the cancer he had started.
But he sure as hell had reasons,
and God damn all the reasons
for which we hurt the children.

I have a fantasy that I was there
when she was flung and followed
quickly over and somehow
caught and held her before we met the water.
That's an empty gesture and quite impossible;
it's just my way of saying
that I'm sorry that he tossed her
like a sack of garbage,
when the very least he might have done
was hold her until the ocean did the parting.

There is a consolation I can offer:
I feel all of us are falling toward the water.
What I don't know is if we jumped,
if something pushed us,
or if the bridge has crumbled.

And something else consoling:
she's
no
longer
plunging
through
this
world
in
which
daddies
throw
their
babies
from
the
bridges.

Flight

Margaret Raymond

Daddy Bud did something bad to mom in their bedroom, then my little brother said something from the hall. "Bud!" I heard mom chop out, not loud but hard. I didn't see it. My throat closed the way it still does when I'm afraid. I went back to sleep.

I woke to the sound of crows. For two days they had covered the thousand-acre bean field. When invaded, they fluttered or lifted, a few at a time. Mom called it a migration. They talked among themselves, pecked, strutted, and kept secret judgment in their yellow eyes. I thought they had decided to leave.

I lay in a tall room on a folding canvas cot. It wrapped itself up my arms and pinned them against my sides. In the cot next to mine, my little brother slept on. He still smelled of dirt even when he was clean, so we were very young; eight and ten or so. He slept late because he had bad dreams the night before and mom had to come in for him. Looking beyond his cot, I saw my dressing table. That dresser confused me. It had frilly curtained arms that swung open to reveal drawers "for my treasures." That's what mom said. "Treasures." She seemed proud of giving me something of my own. She added a wood chair or stool, I don't remember. I'm sure there was a mirror. I think the mirror was held in the hand, that it didn't stand alone. I had corn silk hair, she said. I wanted to be a cabaret singer like she used to be when I grew up. I didn't much care whether I had a mirror or a place for my treasures; I kept my favorite things in my hand or under my pillow for the two or three weeks until Daddy Bud got so drunk we had to move again. Then I threw them away as if I were mad.

Anyway, I woke to the sound of stirring and muttering crows. Some of the night was caught above the picture rail molding in our room, except by the window, where it was grey. I remembered about my brother's nightmare cries; they sounded like a baby's. I should have helped him, I thought. I put on my dress; it lay on the foot of my cot. My socks and shoes were by the closet, so I sat on the floor to put them on. I shivered from cold on my way to the kitchen. I passed mom and Daddy Bud's open bedroom door quickly without peering in. The kitchen was warm from the stove and mom was making pancakes.

"Stay here," she said.

But I went out the kitchen door and down the steps, until I was under the rubber tree where I could watch the crows.

The rubber tree stood just where a tree should be by a house, near to the northeast corner. Its top was rounded just the way a tree's top should be, like an upside-down bowl, and its shade was the right black even on a sunny day. That morning its shade was cold, but that made no difference, because the morning was cold everywhere. There were no crows in the rubber tree; they kept away from buildings. In the field, they were not billowing, just talking, blackening the ground and ready to leave. The sky was flat gray all the way down to where it met the migrating flock. When the sun rose it would be at the height of my face.

My little brother came out the kitchen door and ran down the steps, thud-thud, and then past the tool shed where we practiced our magic tricks. He yelled and waved his arms and ran right into the field of crows. "You can't hit my mom!" he screamed. They finally billowed, then bunched thinly into the sky, and my little brother kept on running, raising a blanket of birds into the air and running, running, a skinny little boy of eight, running and whooping and running and waving his arms between bean-field clods and a sky made black with living, cawing birds not quite ready to really fly away.

He's Not Abusive
Spirette Dotter

An adapted excerpt from Dotter's memoir, entitled
Unlost Truths: A Survivor's Journey Forward

He staggered into the house reeking of alcohol, carrying a bottle in a paper bag.

"Hi, Prinschess."

"You're drunk. *Please* leave." I spoke calmly, firmly.

"Not going anywhere. Brought-cha money. Don'tcha pr-preciate any-anything?"

"You broke our agreement." I glared at him. "You *have* to go."

"Shut up." He pranced into the bathroom, faced the corner farthest from the toilet, and pissed on the floor. "Clean that up."

"*You* clean it. I'm leaving." I filled the diaper bag, then started toward the crib for the babies.

Bill blocked me, his eyes radiating fury. "You b-better *not* go."

"You threatening me?" I froze, staring.

He lifted the coffee table, upside-down, above his head and yelled. "I'll show ya threatening. How'd ya like me ta break this to a m-million pieces, huh?" Feet apart, nostrils flared, he stood huffing, holding the table in the air.

The showdown continued as he waited for my response, until Jeremy cried, and I broke eye contact. I dashed around Bill, scooped up the howling boys and raced outside. I heard a loud crash inside, but didn't look back.

"Don't worry," I said in the car, after catching my breath. "Papa's confused. We'll be fine." Trembling, I locked the doors, then fumbled, trying to jam the key into the ignition.

Who *was* that monster, I wondered, while driving. He's never acted like that.

Still shaky, parked near a payphone, I played with the babies, considering options.

I called the crisis line.

"Are you in a safe place?" the domestic violence advocate

asked.

After a short conversation, we met at Denny's Restaurant.

"How old *are* these little angels?" she asked, smiling.

"Jeremy's twenty-six months. Tivon's eleven months."

"Bill's not abusive, he's an alcoholic." I steadied the boys as they played—climbing up and sliding down our booth. "He's never hit us. Well...he almost hit Jeremy once—scared him till he fell backwards—I don't *think* he hit him. He shoved me once because I got in his way. I was holding newborn Jeremy; his little head got banged on the doorway. Bill didn't mean it. He was drunk. Oh, and once he beat his dog. I didn't see it, but Jake yelped awful and was bruised purple and swollen the next day. I've seen rage in Bill's eyes before. I left because I didn't know what he'd do. He was acting crazy, and he...he threatened me."

I quivered, breathing deeply. "We get along great, when he's not drinking. He's kindhearted, caring, fun—usually. I grew up with a violent rage-aholic father. Bill's nothing like that."

"Most abusers *are* charming. They're cons. They have good qualities, too. That's what hooks us. Are you afraid of your husband?" Brushing her brunette hair back, she searched my eyes.

"He scared me today. I'm jumpy and need to stay near the restroom. Can't believe he threatened me. It's not *like* him. It's the alcohol. Problem is, he can't stay sober."

"Addiction often plays a role in domestic violence." Her forehead winkled. "Victim-batterer cycles are progressive. They only get worse. How long have you been married?"

"Three years. Yeah, it's getting worse. He'd disappear when drunk at first, and never scared me."

"We want you and your children safe. I'll get you into our emergency women's shelter. We'll provide food, clothing, short-term shelter, and help you sort this out. Okay?"

I stared at the boys. "It's their bedtime. Sounds like my best option."

After agreeing to keep the location confidential and not contact Bill, I followed her to a quiet residential area and parked in a driveway behind a fence.

In her office, we finished the intake interview, including questions about my family history. I signed paperwork and received literature about domestic violence. She went over the house rules and chores, then showed me around.

The house was large, newly remodeled, with few residents. I settled into a bedroom and put the babies down for the night.

Can't sleep, I thought, walking toward low voices in the den.

Watching the news on a large console TV, a young woman wearing a robe relaxed on one couch.

I sat on the empty sofa. "Hi. I'm here with my two babies. Been here long?"

"A week. I'm Dana. My boyfriend put me in the hospital. Ten stitches." She pointed to the side of her head, dark hair shaved, cheek bruised.

"Yowch. Glad you're safe and taking care of yourself now." I smiled.

"Yeah, but I miss him," she said. "Wish I could drop the charges, but it's not my choice anymore. Been crying all day, wanting to call him."

"My husband scared us, but he's not abusive. If he ever hurt us, that'd be it. I'd be done. I won't live with violence like my mom did—can't have that for *my* boys. If Bill *is* getting violent, I should take the boys and move away. That'd serve him right."

We talked for hours, until I said goodnight, exhausted. Snuggling in bed near my boys, I thought, "After all she's been through, how can Dana still love her boyfriend?"

Days later, I took the babies on a road trip, looking for a new home. I need to detach—get a fresh start, I thought. But...I already miss him. If he could *only* stay sober....He didn't *mean* to scare us....He's probably sorry now. Least he *only* scared us and wasn't *abusive*. I *should* divorce him anyway and move on. But...it's not that easy. Wish I could let go, but I still love him too much. And the way the boys light up and play with him when he's around. They adore him. If we move far, he'll never find us. What if I divorce him, then he gets better? We can't lose our chance of being a healthy family....I can't *completely* give up hope. Not yet.

Victim Witness

Zara Raab

For a young mother, what terror
lies in her man's violence,
she his constant threshing floor,
the plate glass of a flying chair,
trembling lintel above a door.

And how much worse for her
child who listens at the door,
crouches in a corner, cowers
in her bed beneath the covers
through a sound-track of fear.

Sitting in the darkened theater,
observing from an upper tier,
she learns by heart her mother's
dramas, learns them inside out:
witness to the family war.

Even if her mother dismisses
her own pain, loss reclassified
as lesson—I don't know why—
still, that baleful existence
the child must own before she dies.

I Want Out

Joshua Byrd

A dying breed cries a creed as it bleeds
Can you hear it?
I want out

Young tears shout
in place of their broken spirits
Hopeless lyrics paint illusions
Honeys cars and cash
Total enslavement
They're now addicted to the radio's blast

Miscasted seed in the city facing years down the road
not because he wanted to
but because he was told
that school wasn't cool
He broke the rules as he worked on the block
serving crack to kill his neighbors
as he struggled with pot
I want out

His spirit screamed
but he couldn't let his face know
'cause peer pressure was on his back
His reputation couldn't fold
so he call her a ho
the one he loved with his soul
and she responded to him
'cause no one was there to show
her the way

Mom worked all day
a struggling single
fed up with her baby daddy
'cause every night he would mingle
in the streets

with phony fellas who was jealous of him
because he had a family who really cared about him
    I want out

Mama would scream
with her daughter on her side
to the top of her lungs she would yell
then run and hide
Over my dead body
her baby daddy would say
as he delivered deadly punches that discolored her face
    I want out

Her daughter cried to deaf ears in her home
but mama couldn't hear her cry
'cause she was screaming all along
The cell phone was there to listen
and baby girl had to vent
Ho, what you want
around the fellas
is how her boyfriend would begin

I need you
I want out
I got to get out of this place
Daddy's gone
Mama's home trying to nurse a broken face
He don't love us anymore
He always beats her and leaves
then visits with this sick lady who lives just up the street

It's alright
Come stay with me
because I want you out too
I'm staying with my boy now
but he'll let us use a room

So she went
reluctantly
A week later she would hate

the decision that she made
that caused her to be raped

Now
upset with fate
she gained weight and lost all pride
Pregnant now as a teen
and too ashamed to even cry
    I want out

She screamed inside
but she couldn't let her boyfriend know
that the baby wasn't his
because the baby gave him hope
but she had to
'cause every sleepless night after the rape
her boyfriend's boy
would have his way with her

Shut up
You staying at my place
Pain on her face
pain in her waist
and pain in her heart
had her shaking as she cried
    I want out

In the dark
life was hard
She left the house for life on the boulevard
trying to keep her head up as she prayed to the stars
And then a car
Out of nowhere
snatched her up as she walked

Ho, what you doing?
Is you stupid?
Ho, I'm taking you home
    Baby hold on
No! Here's the phone

Now go ahead and call ya mama
She going through too much right now
She don't need no extra drama
    I don't care
You going home
My boy told me what you did
Y'all had sex
    He raped me
    and this baby is his

His face dropped
He tried to pick it up but it was too heavy
Another blow to a broken spirit
and boy was this scary
    Let me out
    Let me out
But I want to know the truth
Ho, if you lying to me
I swear that I will kill you
    I'm not lying
    I promise you
    He raped me the same night
    That y'all two had an argument
    Over the bet on the fight
    Stop the car
    Right now
    Man, I said let me out

He was heated
He grabbed his piece
as flames poured from his snout
Betrayed by his boy
the hope he had wasn't his
and as the radio blasted
he thought of blasting his friend

Pride began to overtake the little reason he had left
and as the car raced to a halt
he did his best to catch his breath
One finger rested on the trigger

tears rushed to escape his eyes

Open the door
Nigga come out
She standing here right here outside
Now, which one of y'all gone lie to me tonight
'cause I swear
both of y'all can die and sleep tonight
    Man why you trippin' like this
    Over a ho that you don't like
    She ain't nothing, look at her
    and plus I thought we was cool
    I didn't think that you would mind sharing an old piece of news
Man I love her
She's my girl
    Well you should have let me know
Man you knew
    No I didn't
Man I should blast you both
I can't take this shit

And then
with great wind a voice screamed out
Sir put down your gun
but not before
the gun said
Pow
and took him out

A lost teen
a bastard kid who never had a chance to sprout
his whole life he was boxed in
and all he wanted was out

His girlfriend wanted out too
but nobody was there to listen
and her mother wanted out too
of her abusive condition

Her father wanted out of the relationship

that he and his baby's mama had
but no one was there to listen
so he'd beat her when he got mad

If daddy could've expressed his feelings when he was upset
then he wouldn't have beaten the greatest woman he'd ever met
and in turn his child's mother could've listened to her daughter
who was crying for help
as she witnessed the slaughter
of her self esteem and dreams
a single child with no direction
and maybe then she would've stayed
at home and never got pregnant
by a boy who couldn't be a man
because he'd never been taught
and maybe then
she could have lived a life without
claiming the fault
of him
going out too early

A bastard kid in the city
who never had a chance to sprout
boxed in his whole life
and all he wanted was out

Eating in Silence
David Rosas

My four brothers had already eaten and went to feed the cows, goats, chickens, and pigs. Taking their seats at the living room table, we ate dinner in silence. Daddy wasn't home. He normally returned from work, but today he didn't. *Mamí* seemed worried. I could feel her uneasiness while she served dinner to my sisters and me. We ate *arroz, frijoles, pescado frito y tortillas de harina*. Because we were Catholics, we always had fish on Fridays. Being the youngest girl at six, I was served first by *mi Mamí* because I am "*la baby.*"

"Where's Daddy?" I asked *Mamí*.

She replied in a quiet voice, her head and brown eyes turned downward, "*Sylvia, el está en la cantina.*"

"*¿La cantina?*" I asked.

She replied quickly in a nervous tone. "*Sí, La Cucaracha. Una cantina cerca de la escuela. Come tu cena y no mas preguntas.*"[1]

I knew when Daddy drank too much. He turned into *el diablo*, one I had seen before and was afraid of.

We went to bed early in our little two-bedroom house. My brothers, Joe, Danny, Tony, and David, slept in the crooked house that my Dad built for the boys behind the main house. Our bedroom was off the living room. Rosa slept in a twin bed. I slept on the bottom bunk bed and Shirley slept on the top. I don't remember what time *mi Mamí* crawled into my bed, but I loved cuddling with her.

I was asleep when Daddy drove down Billington Lane, our dusty dirt road, off of Hembree Lane. We heard him open the front door and walk into his bedroom. He realized that *Mamí* was not there.

"*¡Maria! ¡Maria! ¿Dónde estás? ¿Con tu novio?*"[2] he yelled.

My sister Rosa swung the silver-colored door latch into the little metal eye loop attached to the doorjamb to lock the door.

"*Aquí estoy.*" *Mamí* called back in an anxious voice, rising from the bed.

"*¡Salga del cuarto!*"[3] he screamed through the door.

"*No, Jose. Estás borracho,*" *Mamí* replied. "*Hablaremos mañana. Duérmete.*"[4]

¡Pinche puta! ¡Abre la puerta! [5] he roared.

"*No José. Tu no estás bien. Mañana.*"

He walked to his bedroom off the kitchen. But soon we heard his heavy railroad boots pounding through the kitchen and back toward our bedroom door.

"Bam!" The door busted open, taking the latch and loop with it. *Mamí* jumped into my bed, hugging me tightly. He reached for her, holding a black, leather whip in his other hand.

"*¡Venga pinche mujer!*" he belted out.

"*¡Nooooo Jose! ¡Nooooo Jose!*" *Mamí* cried.

Daddy raised the whip and brought it down on her. She turned her back and hugged me, to protect me and brace for the whip that struck her on the back. She screamed in pain next to my ear. Her body shook. She braced for another lash. My sisters and I were crying and our terrified screams filled the room.

The rhythm of her body shook every time the leather connected with her back and our screaming became the background chorus.

Shirley jumped from the top bunk and landed on Daddy's back, wrapping her arms around his neck, trying to strangle him. Daddy slowed down his whipping and turned his attention to his daughter.

"*¡Pinche muchacha!*" he roared.

Shirley distracted him long enough for *Mamí* to jump from the bed and run out the door. He staggered after her, whipping her over and over. Shirley's white and pink nightgown waved as she clung to him. She rode him like a *vaquera* on a wild bull.

Shirley was only thirteen and no match for him. He reached back, pulled her long black hair, and threw her to the ground. He punched her, knocking her on the floor. She lay motionless.

Rosa and I made for the bedroom door, but the drunken devil cut us off. Rosa used me as a shield to protect herself from him. She held tightly onto my two-piece flannel PJs. We stood motionless.

"*¿Donde fue tu Mamá?*" he asked.

"We don't know," we replied. Tears flowed down our pale cheeks. We froze, waiting for the whip, but then he ran out and checked the bathroom, looking for *Mamí*. He stormed out to the crooked house, yelling at the boys,

"*¿Dónde está tu Mamá?*"

"Shit, we don't know!" the boys yelled. The boys were asleep and unaware of what had happened in the little house minutes earlier.

"*¿Están escondiendo a tu Mamá?*[6]" he yelled.

"No!" the boys yelled, still oblivious to the situation.

He left the boys and made his way to his car, started the engine, and drove off.

My brothers came into the house to find Shirley lying on the old cracked, vinyl floor. Rosa and I held each other in the bed, hiding under the covers, crying. My two older brothers, Joe and Danny, picked up Shirley and gently put her in the lower bunk bed.

With tears running down her face, Rosa described what happened. Her voice trembled as she relived the terror. The seven of us waited in silence, abandoned by our parents at the end of Billington Lane.

Finally, my fifteen-year-old brother Joe said, "Everything will be fine. Go back to bed. Tomorrow is Saturday. Mom will come back tomorrow."

Rosa and I cried ourselves to sleep. We heard Daddy come home just before dawn. We woke up when he opened the front door. His footsteps echoed throughout the house and then we heard his drunken snores fill the air.

Mamí returned later in the morning. She had escaped by running across town to *Tío* Sarafin's house, Daddy's elder brother. He came with *mi Tía* Reina and *Mamí*. *Tía* and *Mamí* stayed in the car and *Tío* Sarafin came into the house. He spoke with Daddy for a while. Daddy emerged from the bedroom remorseful, tired, and hung over.

Tío Sarafin went to the car to talk to *Mamí*. She got out and spoke with Daddy, then trudged into the house and started his breakfast.

When the boys were outside working in the garden, and feeding the animals, and my Daddy was running errands in town, *Mamí* showed her daughters her back. The red welts across her white skin reminded me of pirate movies when a captain has a sailor whipped. Rosa, Shirley, and I looked on feeling powerless. I couldn't understand why the man I called Daddy could turn into the devil and cause us so much pain.

The family settled into the farm and family routine that Saturday. Daddy was home. We ate dinner in silence.

[1] Yes, the Cockroach. A bar near the school. Eat your dinner and no more questions.
[2] Where are you? With your boyfriend?
[3] Come out of the room.
[4] We'll talk tomorrow. Go to sleep.
[5] Fuckin' whore! Open the door!
[6] Are you hiding your mother?

The Knife
Farrell Winter

Morning.
A dull pain in my stomach.
Not digestive juice churning
this time.
A spot of blood
the knife clutched in my hand,
taken from the silverware drawer
last night
after everyone had gone to bed,
the yelling stopped,
the heavy air beginning to settle
a little.
"I'll hold this knife all night,"
I said—
silently of course,
so he wouldn't hear.
To protect myself
in case he comes in
to hit me.
"I'll cut his arms off
if he raises his fist at me."
Cut cut cut.
"I'll stab him in the chest
but it won't hurt him
because he has no heart."
Stab stab stab.
How could he have a heart
and beat his own son
daily?
Every day
these past ten years,
since the day he returned from the war
against America's enemies.
Now I'm America's enemy
and he's still at war.

That evil smile on his face
as he took off his belt,
doubled it up
and pulled me across his lap,
his words
repeated incessantly
like a madman.
"I told you not to do that.
I told you. I told you. I told you."
I never knew what.
"This hurts me more than it hurts you."
Then why do it, I thought.
Finally deciding
he liked being hurt.
"I'll hit you so hard
you'll feel it next week."
Why are you hitting that little boy,
I thought
watching from over my shoulder.
My mother intervened
on occasion.
"You hit him enough today," she'd say,
"Hit him again tomorrow."
or simply, "Stop hitting him."
"I'm not hitting him.
You don't see any blood, do you?"
My pain and fear
eclipsed by terror.
But he never made me bleed.
Now I make myself bleed
with this knife.

Two years later
when my mother said,
"Stop hitting him,"
and he responded,
"I'm not hitting him,"
she said—
"You hit him before he was born."
I had this vision:

A young couple
newly married.
He comes home
from a day of looking for work.
"Oh, Phil,"
she gurgles happily.
"I'm pregnant."
He looks at her,
begins punching her stomach,
screaming,
"You love the baby more than me,"
over and over,
like a madman.

Now,
this morning,
he throws open my door
and looks at me
with the evil smile,
searching for an excuse.
I hold up the knife
and shout, "Keep away"
in my mind.
In reality
I keep the knife hidden
lest he see it
and give me the beating of my life.
Again.

Strangled

Ann Hutchinson

My husband, Ron, and his brother Micky came home late from a night of drinking. Micky, who was visiting, brought along a girl from the bar. Having my drunken husband come to bed and expect sex was bad enough, but I couldn't bear the thought of Micky having sex with some chick in the living room. So, I tossed a blanket and pillow out to the hallway for Ron and locked the bedroom door, reasoning that Micky wouldn't have sex in my living room with Ron there. Outraged, Ron started cursing and banging on the door. Our only phone was in the kitchen, so I couldn't call the police.

"Open this door right now, or I'll break it down!" Terrified, I jumped out the window. I fled blindly away through the parking lot and down the driveway to save myself and my unborn child. My heart beat even faster as I realized there was nowhere to run. The darkened businesses that surrounded our apartment complex mocked me. Where did I think I was going to go?

I turned back and ran to the upstairs neighbor's apartment and pelted their door with my fists. Before Quinton answered, Ron grabbed me and hauled me back downstairs. He threw me on the bed and wrapped his hands around my throat, pinning me down. I couldn't believe he was choking me, his pregnant wife, with our daughter in her crib in the next room and Micky and Quinton standing in the hallway watching. Struggling for breath, I pounded on his arms. He squeezed tighter. I thought those red eyes would be the last things I saw, the stench of alcohol and rage the last things I smelled. My vision turned into a field of incomprehensible dots like snow on a TV with no signal. Was he really going to kill me?

Then I heard more voices and a police radio. "Ron, the police are here," Quinton said from the hallway.

Finally, my crazed husband eased the pressure on my throat. I felt the blood returning to my head in a rush. He got off me and stepped away. I rubbed my sore neck. My vision returned. I didn't look at Ron. I didn't need another look at the scary, red eyes of a raging beast. Instead, I scanned the room. The heavy, wooden easy chair was upside down and, four feet up the wall, was a hole the size and shape of the chair's leg.

How did I end up married to such an abusive man? He didn't act like this when we met. But even then, plenty of red flags were there if I had only been paying attention. But, after losing my Dad to leukemia when I was sixteen, I was desperate to fill the void he'd left. That's why I entered a relationship with Ron. That, and I thought marrying the man I had premarital sex with would lessen my sin. I could say that what I did wasn't really so bad, just bad timing—done out of order. Weren't girls who got pregnant pushed into marrying the father? Whose shame were the parents trying to hide?

Why don't our parents tell us they did the same things when they were young and it's not the end of the world, that it's not an unforgivable sin? I wasn't even pregnant. I could have walked away. I married Ron out of a warped sense of loyalty.

Nine months after Ron strangled me, I finally did walk away. I was waiting for him to wake up after his methamphetamine crash. I had let him con me out of the food stamps again the night before—the food stamps we were on because he wouldn't get a job. He knew how to play the loyalty card. "How can I show you I've changed unless you give me a chance?" he would say. I'd been waiting to get groceries, but I knew he had done it again— exchanged the food stamps for drugs.

I had no friends; I couldn't let anyone know the hell I lived in. After leaving my daughter with my mother, I went to Micky's house with my five-month-old son, Wesley, to see if his girlfriend, Charlotte, was there. We were friends of a sort. She wasn't there, but Micky said she'd be home from work shortly and why didn't I go with them to the fair? That sounded like a lot more fun than hearing my tweaker husband make excuses again for why he didn't have the food stamps. When Charlotte returned, I left Wesley with her while I went back to the apartment for more diapers.

Ron was awake and angry. He demanded to know where I'd been. I told him. He grabbed my arms so hard he bruised them. Then he threw me against the wall, all the while screaming at me and calling me names. As I left with the diapers, he yelled after me, for all the neighbors to hear, that I was a whore and sleeping with his brother.

Years later, I began to understand how I could accept outrageous behavior as normal, and live isolated and under siege for so long. I understand now about the addictions that took over my ex-husband and my disease of co-dependency that kept me trapped in a destructive relationship.

What I still don't understand, twenty-six years later, is why Quinton and Micky only pleaded with Ron to let me go while I was being strangled; why two grown men wouldn't help me. Maybe they suffered from misplaced loyalty, too.

Tippy's Tail
Louise Young

Terry eases through the warped screen door, holding it so it won't slam, and sits on the top step of the concrete porch. The house looks tiny sandwiched among rows of desolate warehouses. Heat radiates off the pavement. All the windows are open, waiting for a breeze, but have no screens to keep the flies out.

I sit still in my car and watch. Terry holds a tan, stuffed dog, worn bare in spots. Its tail flops oddly toward one front leg, hanging on by a thread. He crouches over the dog and begins to rock as if to comfort it. He's nine, slight in build, with delicate features set in a face marked with unrelieved sadness. He sits quietly, like an old person living in the past. His teacher said he seems indistinct, as if his life story is being recorded in ink that fades with time.

I've had one visit with Mrs. Harper, her son Terry, and his stepfather, Emery. I asked Terry a few questions about friends and school, but his mother did all the talking. According to her, everything is rosy with her family. All I could do for Terry that day was smile at him and say, "See you next week."

Suddenly a woman's scream crashes through the air, bounces off the buildings and pavement and smacks my ears with a tsunami of rage.

Oh, my God, no. Not this, not now. I start to sweat and shake. My breath comes in gasps. I am seven again.

My mother is screaming and dishes are smashing. She picks up the broom and comes after me. I fall over myself running. I hide behind the hydrangea by the front door with the spiders and dead leaves. The broom handle sails like a javelin by me, inches from my face. If I don't move, don't make a sound, she won't find me.

It was years before I understood that I was not her target, only a stand-in for some ghost from her past. It wasn't me; it wasn't my fault. But the feelings are still the same. Will I ever be finished with this?

I'm paralyzed with panic. I want to leave before Terry notices me. He is still rocking, now bent over his tattered dog, drawing it closer to his body.

Then a woman's raspy yelling floods the space around the house. "God damn son of a bitch, I'll break every bone in your body, you do that again, you hear me? You ever hit me or Terry again I'll kill you. I got a gun and I'll shoot your arms off, you hit him again."

A male voice hollers, "The little shit was getting into my stuff. You keep him outta my room. I don't want that effin' cry-baby anywhere near me."

"You don't like it here, get the hell out; get your stuff and get out now."

The rage has dissolved into an argument, and I stop hearing them. My panic is over, but I'm dead tired. I can't help this little boy now. I need to go home and sleep.

Can I tell Terry that soon he will be big enough to leave, like I did? That if he is patient and careful, someday he will have his own space and not have to live with crazy people? But he needs help now.

OK, think. I went into social work to give kids like Terry hope that there's at least one adult in the world who could understand, be a friend. Now Terry rests his cheek against the dog, cradling it close to his chest.

My eyes flick to the dog. Of course. There is something I can do, that a friend would do. I can't fix Terry, but I can fix the dog's tail. I dig in my bag for my travel sewing kit and take a deep breath.

When I leave the car, Terry recognizes me. I walk a few steps and stop, as if I've just now seen him. I smile. "Hi, Terry," I say. He straightens and his eyes meet mine, alert, waiting.

I walk to the steps. "May I sit here?" He nods. I sit next to him, but not too close. "That's a cute dog there. Had him long?" I ask.

Terry nods, and says softly, "I got him when I was born."

"What's his name?"

"Tippy," he says firmly. Yes, the end of Tippy's tail was once white.

"Looks like Tippy's tail is loose."

"Whew! That's Emery. He grabbed Tippy by his tail, and it tore. Then he threw Tippy against the wall, hard."

"Ooooh, he was mad, huh?"

"Yeah, Tippy should've bit him."

Oh. I see. Do I play along? Terry is nine. He will soon need all the reality he can muster. "Oh," I say. "I meant Emery. Emery must have been mad."

"Oh, Emery. He's always mad, AND he hates me."

"That must be hard."

Terry looks me in the eye for the first time. I wonder if anyone has ever believed him.

"Hey, Terry. I think I could fix Tippy's tail." I show him my sewing kit. "I could sew it on, if you want."

"You could?"

"I'm pretty sure I could." I reel off some tan thread and clip it. I pretend to have difficulty threading the needle. I could thread a needle in the dark, but I need to enlist Terry into the project. "Could you thread it?"

"Sure. I do it for my grandma sometimes." Ah, another player in this family drama.

I say, "Is there shade anywhere? It's really hot out here."

"We could go out front. It's shady there."

"Let's."

A sagging porch offered a tiny patch of shade over the single front step. We sit, and I reach for Tippy.

Terry gives Tippy a squeeze and hands him over. "There's a torn place on his stomach, too. Could you fix that after his tail?"

"Yes, I think so."

House of Mirrors
Janet Vallance

He is at once Superman and afraid of intimacy. He screams in our faces and charms the neighbors in the same afternoon. Everyone thinks he is amazing. Everyone thinks he is such a great dad. He treats you like a prostitute and you are trying like hell to please him. He can never be pleased. If the small lies get bigger, if what you saw and what he says no longer lines up—start a serious savings account.

It really did happen.

Your children are learning how to behave from his actions. There is no amount of money that can reverse that damage. Form a bond with a sheriff, get on a first name basis with the DA. Put the Domestic Violence hotline on speed dial marked as "Joan."

You would lie down in traffic for your children. He can never take that away. There is a bunk bed in hell with his name on it. Do not be afraid. You are a protected child of God. No matter what your religion—you are a Mother and a gift and you will have what you need. He is full of feathers and dung. You are full of flesh and bone and the infinite power of love.

Dawn

"And the day came when the risk to remain tight in a bud was more painful than the risk it took to blossom."

—Anaïs Nin

Body on the Wall
Michelle Wing

They send me a slip of paper
Anger Management—Certificate of Completion
And his name.
As if.

As if twelve weeks of one-hour sessions,
of talking about his feelings,
of tips on counting to ten,
could make him into a new man—

could undo the damage.

I know too well he can con anyone:
Police. Lawyers. Landlords.
Me.

And this piece of paper is the last slap
I am ever going to feel.

I walk to my closet, and get my dancing dress,
the little black one that twirls when I move,
that reminds me of freedom and the time before.

Do you want to know what he is like?
I'll need some tools.

Scissors to slash the hemline.
Blades to rip open sleeves.

A lighter to torch the fluttering strips.
Dirty boots to grind out the flames.

Then a razor, to nick my forearm
so I can smear blood across his name
and pin that piece of paper to my ruined dress.

I bandage my arm, find a hanger—

It is my body on the wall, bruised and battered,
and nobody, nobody, can say they don't see.

A Woman in Search of God

(Excerpt from April 4, 2005)
Diane Madrigal

I watched the clouds gather overhead. Rain was near.

The children sat quietly watching a video. This had been a hard week—nightmares, anger, pain, and sorrow. They missed their father. And when he went away, most of his family did also. Thirty relatives, including cousins, aunts, uncles, their brother, and a grandpa, just receded like the tide. The loss was great.

Julie's fifth birthday was next week. It would be a quiet one.

It had been nine months since he attacked us, but it felt like it had happened that morning. Watching my children suffer left me desperate and without words. How do you explain the unimaginable?

Flashbacks flooded my unguarded moments. I was holding back so much, trying to keep from falling apart. My heart sank deep inside, as my voice did. The questions in my mind kept whirling like the leaves in a coming storm. Never answered.

I kept playing the scenario out in my mind, trying to figure out what I could have done differently to stop him. And every time, I was left with the aftermath, where we are now: devastated.

The girls snuggled down into their fuzzy blankets for a little un-resisted nap. I prayed that they were too exhausted to dream.

I donned my husband's old rain jacket, big garden boots and gloves. With the girls asleep, this would be the best time to get the trash barrels out.

As the breeze blew with a gust, the trees and plants seemed to move like an ocean wave to the shore. The colors of the yard were loud, vibrant, and alive. Yet, there were no voices to be heard.

I had spent the long night before going through several boxes in the garage. I found memories of the last five years that now seemed foreign. Trying desperately to separate him from my soul, I began filling the barrels in a frenzy, as if somehow I could erase what had happened.

I wanted to shout in anger, but no sound came from my lips. Instead, my screams exploded deep inside, tearing away the moments of our life when life was good. To have died would have hurt less. What happened to us? I struggled with the hate for the man he had become and the grief for the man I had loved and lost.

I pulled those barrels, that weighed me down like anchors, to the edge of curb. I left them for the trash man to bury.

I had to go on...for the children. I needed to be strong.

When I hurried to the backyard to bring out the last barrel, it began to rain. A soft mist touched my cheek, a welcomed sense of coolness to my face, warm with anger. I walked into the garden as if I were walking into a place that had no time, distant and far away, disconnected from the rest of the world, offering me solace. Even in its neglected state, it welcomed me like an old friend.

I could see that tall weeds had taken over my garden. I reached down to pull one and it snapped in two. I grabbed further down the stem. Again it snapped.

The rain changed from a mist to racing drops. My heart ached. Tears came. "It was just a weed!" I told myself. I reached down to the base, and with a firm grip, I pulled. I could feel the resistance of this plant as if it was pulling back, but I did not let go. I pulled slowly and steadily, past its resistance until it gave way. The weed came out, root and all. I stood there looking at it. Instead of being uprooted, it allowed itself to be torn away.

I began to pull them with a vengeance, yanking them from the base and throwing them onto the pavement. My body trembled with anger and exploded with anguish. I couldn't give up hope. The skies burst open as I yelled into the rain, "No! You can't take my garden!" I stood in the midst of the enemy, the rainwater swirling around my boots, soaking into the ground. They were like an army; some had thorns and were sticking to my mud-covered gloves. The weeds were shrieking back from my grasping hands. "Get out!" I yelled.

The voice of a wounded child emerged from the core of my being, crying out with the deepest hurt and uncontrollable pangs of truths into the deafening rain. I cried for my family, my children, my husband. "Why?"

My mind filled with prayer.

Whispering, so only God could hear me, I prayed, "Please, Father, please. Please, Father. Help me!" The whole world disappeared.

A burst of energy came upon me. I saw my hands pulling faster and faster. The weeds were jumping right out of the ground! I gave all I had left.

I became aware of the silence. It was still raining, raining hard. But this silence...I stood there—just breathing, waiting...as if I would hear God's voice call out to me.

The most amazing peace settled over me. Warmth embraced and surrounded me. God was here. He knew my pain. For the first time since the attack, my thoughts quieted.

God was showing me that I had strength to go on—to do what I had to do. That He would be with me. I finally understood.

"Thank you, Father, for the strength you give me to pull the weeds from my garden. For allowing me to surrender my pain, my hurts, my hate, my anger. Thank you for your love and mercy, for your comfort and Grace, for saving my children, sparing my life, for giving me hope and courage to go on, for teaching me to trust You."

I stepped back. I could see my path. There was still work to be done, but I now had hope that I would see my garden in the Spring.

Fear to Fierceness: Divine Wisdom

Dianna L. Grayer

I. As I Wait for the Sound

The screaming.
The yelling.
Make them stop.
Please God make them stop.

The crashing.
The tussling.
Please make them stop.
Will somebody stop them.

The cursing.
The loudness.
Bodies hit the wall.
Door crashes open.
Echoes surround me.

This familiar image before me.
Do they not see me?
Do they not hear me?
Do they not care about me?

Not the rifle.
Both gripping the barrel.
Neither letting go.
Venom outlining their faces.

Terror hits me like a weapon.
First to my heart.
Then to my head.
The biggest blow to my gut.
My life knocked out of me.

Soul loss.

Somewhat awake.
But mostly I'm gone.
The only way I survive.

I lose my vision.
They disappear.
But I have my ears.
I whimper, powerless.

I pray steadily.
Exhausted, but still standing.
As I wait for the sound.
As I wait for the sound.
As I wait for the sound.

II. Now I Stand Before You

Now I stand before you stronger and wiser
having moved through the darkness.
No longer victim.
No longer powerless.
No longer waiting.

But offering,
teaching,
empowering,
healing.

I'm on a mission to awaken.
To free the spirit
from the suffocating hands of
shame.
Fear.
Self-doubt.
Low self-esteem, and
powerlessness.

I'm committed to do no harm.
With an open, receptive, and compassionate heart.

I'm embraced by the wisdom and guidance of my
guides,
angels,
teachers,
ancestors,
Creator God
and Mother Earth,
all who feed my soul.

Now I stand before you
as healer.
Never forgetting the pain and anguish
that moves in me,
that which inspires me to move.
To be active—not reactive.

Now I stand before you
more fierce than ever.
Soaring with eagle.

Now I stand before you
basking in the light.
It shines on me.
And runs through me.
And flows out of me.

And touches You.

Now I stand before you.

In *Cry of the Nightbird: Writers Against Domestic Violence*, thirty-eight writers speak out in more than fifty prose and poetry pieces of a hidden tragedy: violence in homes, living in fear, and forced silence. Authors from every walk of life and every aspect of this difficult issue raise their voices as one to end this silence, to bring freedom and release for themselves and others. These words will inform and inspire readers: give them eyes to see, a way to express, and motivation to act.

To order more copies:

Sales of *Cry of the Nightbird: Writers Against Domestic Violence* directly fund the domestic violence work of YWCA Sonoma County. To purchase more copies, visit our online store at www.ywcasc.org

Cost: $15 ea. + shipping

Cry of the Nightbird is also available in a Kindle edition on Amazon.com

How I Became a Poet
Michelle Wing

After the hurt, and before the healing, there is rage. If you had asked me to don that cloak, I would have said no. But it falls about my shoulders uninvited, comes to me as I walk the city streets. Fury envelops me.

↑
ⲓⲣⲉ

In an art therapy group, the counselor asks us to take turns lying down on large pieces of butcher-block paper, while someone traces the outline of our bodies with a fat, black marker. Our assignment is to place emotions in the form.

I fill my head with anxiety, dread, despair, depression and suicidality. There is not enough room for all the dark words. I move down to the stomach and chest to add in hurt, lost, scared, alone. I am very aware of the imbalance, the negativity, so I search for something, anything, positive. I look at my right arm, and decide to grace it with my creativity, my desire to write, even if at this moment I am unable to write a single word, except big block letters in an art therapy group.

Almost as an afterthought, I draw a small spiral in my gut, and in tiny controlled print I label it: rage.

↑
ⲓⲣⲉ

The first time I feel its presence I am alone. A well-intentioned friend gives me a videotape of lesbian soft porn shorts. She thinks I need to get rid of the "good girl" image, push the boundaries, put some edge into my life. I take the tape home and put it into the VCR. The third movie is an S&M scene between girlfriends. The dominant woman calls the submissive one ugly, degrading names. The sex looks like rape. I do not care that it is supposedly consensual. It is asking me to find pleasure in exactly the kind of torture I have escaped. I am momentarily frozen. Then I awake, and eject the tape.

It is not enough to throw it away. I go to the kitchen and find a hammer. I smash the case until it is in splinters. I pull out mile after mile of offending tape, until I am sitting in a sea of smut. The destruction helps my body work out its disgust and anger. Completely spent, I walk to the dumpster, trailing my ribbons of despair.

free

I am sitting on the living room floor in a two-story apartment unit with a friend. I hear a man yell abusive, foul language outside. I race to the window, arriving just in time to see this stranger grab his female partner and throw her, hard, onto the concrete.

I am out the door and screaming, in a deep guttural voice, standing on the cement balcony, "Stop!" He ignores me as he kicks her. No. Not again. Not one more. The stairs are too far away. I put my foot up on the railing, ready to catapult myself over the edge. I am caught in mid-air, my arms pinioned behind my back, the whispered words, "No, baby, this isn't the way." My male friend pulls me away from my attempted leap. I am kicking and yelling, but he is stronger than me, and I can only struggle and cry out in his arms.

Neighbors begin to peek out from behind curtains. Someone has called 911. It is too late. The stranger has pushed the woman into a car, and they have driven away.

free

I am in San Francisco at three in the afternoon, near the intersection of 16th and Mission streets. It is sunny, and the sidewalks are filled with pedestrians. As I pass a small shop, the fire escape drops down, and a man and woman descend. It gets my attention. I step back into the shadows to watch. The man hits the concrete first; he is holding the woman's wrist in his hands. She is wearing a short skirt, and her legs and arms are covered in bruises. He pulls her down onto the sidewalk, and then out into traffic. She is trying to yank away from him, pleading with him to let her go. He is dragging her across the street. There are people everywhere. No one looks at them.

I feel the anger rising up in me. I step out between the cars and follow. They head into the alley on the other side, the man forcing her every step. At the opening of the alley, I stand, feet spread apart, hands on hips, and in a huge, booming voice, I call out, "Hey, buddy!" He stops. He turns around and sees me there. I say, "Let her go." He says, "You don't understand." I say, "I don't need to understand anything. Let her go." He hesitates, then lifts his hand up in the air, releases his grip, and the woman flees down the alley. I sense something. I turn my head, and find twenty people gathered behind me, an impromptu back-up gang for my confrontation.

⟆

I am driving in the Mission District, on my way home. I come upon a couple arguing. The woman has take-out food. She is offering it to the man. As I watch, he slaps it out of her hand, onto the pavement. She recoils, then assumes that too-familiar stance of trying to make things right. She picks it up; I hear her apologizing. I pull alongside. "Do you need a ride?" I know it is a risk for both of us. I don't care. She hesitates, and says she's OK. I drive just a little way down the block. The volume of the argument increases. She turns, sees me still there. I recognize the pleading in her eyes. I back up, and swing open the passenger door. He is furious. But she gets into the car, and at least for this moment, this time, she is safe.

⟆

I walk the streets of the city dressed in black, with my black motorcycle boots. I am bristling with rage, because it seems that everywhere I turn, I see batterers. Everywhere I look, I am a witness to men who are abusing women. And I will throw my 118-pound fury directly in their path. I will make them wish they had never met me.

Until finally the day comes when I realize the anger is consuming me instead of serving me. It is eating me up and leaving me bitter, lonely, and fragmented. Although sometimes offering temporary assistance, rather than being truly helpful, my deeds are too often acts of self-exposure, putting me in harm's way again and again, with no thoughts of consequence, no concept of self-love.

With this understanding I am able to move, at last, towards healing. I start to think about surviving, both in a physical sense and in a metaphorical sense. I focus on whom I can become, instead of what has been taken from me. I turn deep into myself and find I have my own reservoir of strength, one that is filled, not with hatred and rage, but with compassion and hope.

I begin to fight my battles with poetry instead of hammers.

I sit down to write.

Sometimes It Sneaks Up On You
Lilith Rogers

I'd been lovers with him, on and off, for several years. We'd had an open relationship during that time. I'd had other men lovers and women, too. During part of that time, I'd even lived with one woman lover, and he'd helped us turn the attic of our little rental house in San Francisco into a bedroom for her and me. He was a self-employed carpenter and his skills always came in handy.

I was in my late twenties when I decided that, if I were going to have another child—my precious little girl from my first serious lover was five and she kept begging me for a brother or sister—I should get on with it. And he was so good with her, I thought he'd be a good daddy. And he wanted a child, too.

But he insisted that if we were going to have a child together we should live together, and that made sense I figured. So my daughter and I moved in with him, and almost immediately things changed.

He kept a much tidier home than I did on my own. He'd complain about there being no empty shelves, no counter space, unfolded laundry on the couch. I figured, well, it is his space, and it is probably good to set a better example for my daughter. So, I tried to always have everything picked up and put away when he came home, and he stopped complaining so much.

Then he also started putting up a fuss about my seeing my woman lover. Said she took up too much of my time and energy, and wasn't he enough for me now? After awhile, I decided it wasn't worth the hassle with him to keep that going, so I told her we'd have to chill out—at least temporarily.

It took longer than I figured it would for me to get pregnant—turned out he had some complications in that department he hadn't mentioned. But after a year or so, I did. By then, we'd moved into a fixer-upper house that both our parents helped us buy. When he wasn't working on other houses, he was working on ours. I was still working part time as a gardener, until I fell off a retaining wall midway through the pregnancy and broke my leg and my wrist. Luckily, my baby stayed right inside and was fine. He wasn't too fine about my being laid up, though, and even went out and got me a little weeding job I could do hobbling around. He insisted I do more of the cooking and other chores now I was home more. Well, I did.

Soon my casts came off and a few weeks later, our darling little daughter was born, at home in our bed, with a midwife to guide her out. He was different about how we should parent her than I thought he would be. He didn't want her sharing our bed, didn't even want her crib next to our bed after only a couple of weeks. She needed to learn to be independent, he said. What? She was a tiny baby! My older daughter had shared the bed and the bedroom with her father and me for a couple of years, and she'd turned out great. But he insisted, and I couldn't resist. I hated to argue with him; he'd lose his temper and yell at me and scare the kids. And me. So, I gave in on that, too.

More and more, we ended up in roles I'd never thought that I, a liberated bisexual feminist woman of the '70s, would take on or allow. I was supposed to be the housewife and mother; he the breadwinner and boss. The kids better know that, too. And I was thinking maybe I'd better start thinking of moving on when— oops—I got pregnant again. And this time we had a little boy.

Did I mention that I was beginning to notice that his alcohol consumption was creeping up? Wine with dinner, a brandy or two afterward? And—when I wasn't pregnant—I was drinking more myself. He lost his temper the more that he drank; I paid less attention to his outbursts the more that I did.

It got to the point I realized I was tense around him most of the time. Afraid he'd yell at me or the kids. Naturally, being kids, they often made a mess, and he was clear with them that messes were not allowed.

Without realizing it in the few years I'd lived with him, I'd gone from being an easygoing, casual cook and housecleaner, independent thinker and doer, fun loving mom and lover, to a nervous, edgy, placating, anxious mother of three kids, feeling more and more isolated. I was stuck in a situation I wasn't happy about, but didn't know how to change. Even though I'd gotten a parttime teaching job in the horticulture department at the local community college, he was still the main wage earner. He never let me forget that he should, therefore, have the main say in how the money was spent.

It came to a head one day when our boy was about three;

the girls were five and twelve. My older daughter was living part time with her dad across town by then—the tension in the household was too much for her. We were having an argument about some stupid thing about dinner, or the unswept floor, or the unfolded laundry, and he threw a plate at me. I ducked and it broke against the wall.

"That's it, I'm out of here!" I shouted. "I can't take this any more. I'm afraid of you; the children are afraid of you. I'm not living like this any longer."

"Come on, it was only a plate. It wouldn't have hurt you if it had hit you, and I missed you on purpose."

"You did not miss me on purpose and whether it had hurt me or not, you have no right to throw things at me, to yell at me, to boss me around all the time. I'm miserable, the kids are miserable—and you're miserable, too. I'm taking them to my folks' house now, and we'll figure out something from there."

We tried after that to work things out in counseling, but he wouldn't budge from his position that it was all my fault. So we separated—thank heavens my folks were able to help find housing for me and the kids, and I got a job.

I realized that I was an alcoholic and he was, too. With the help of AA, I sobered up, but he wouldn't. Then I learned about co-dependency, that I had become a co-dependent with him, and I got help with that, too.

I guess the main thing I realized after some time was that my self-esteem had been whittled, whittled, whittled away. It was years of counseling and rebuilding my self-confidence until I finally got my ego back to the place it had been when I'd moved in with him and allowed him to gradually take over my life.

Sometimes it just sort of creeps up on you. But, if you're lucky as I was, and you have some good helpers, you can figure it out before it's too late to regain the joy and wonder in your life—and your children's lives—that we all deserve.

Ask Any Woman

Vilma Ginzberg

Every woman knows, whether she tells or not,
every woman knows when her soul does not consent;
every woman knows when it's really rape.

No one wants to say the words,
"I have been raped."

It opens a wound that cuts too deep,
that slices into private sanctuaries
where fragile flowers of trust, like orchids in the desert,
require much to live and little to die.

But ask any woman.
Every woman knows when it's really rape.

We are being raped, woman and man alike,
child and elder together,
one by one and *en masse,*
black, white, yellow, red, brown,
nutmeg, cinnamon, and saffron-skinned,
and rainbow too.

Ask any woman.
She knows when she is being used, abused,
even when her mind buys the lies,
her soul knows;
even when her need turns her eyes away,
her soul knows.

In the coffin of her throat,
where embers of outrage lie entombed,
harboring dormant protest,
her soul knows, and waits.

No one likes to say,

"I am being raped by those I have chosen."
The embarrassment weakens the will.

But ask any woman;
every woman knows when it's really rape.

No one wants to say,
"I am being raped by those I need."
The humiliation turns us on ourselves,
envelops us in shame.

But ask any woman;
every woman knows when it's really rape.

Never mind the sweet talk, seducing with pillowing promises.
Never mind the artful distraction
turning our eyes to the beautifully crafted sheath
which ultimately, always, houses the waiting shiv.

But listen:
a heroic few *are* saying "I have been raped!"
And we are finally listening,
for they are singing our soul's dirge.

Do you feel the heat rising in your belly?
Are smoldering embers coming to life?

Do you hear yourself screaming, however softly,
"STOP!" "ENOUGH!" "NO MORE! NO MORE!"

When our fires all have merged, my sisters and brothers,
will it be a controlled burn,
or a raging wildfire devastation?

Meantime, ask *yourself*, and listen;
we *all* know when it's really rape:
the soul knows.

But if you're not sure,
ask any woman.

Hidden Wounds

Peggy Raggio

It was the last day of June 1973. For a year, waiting for the divorce to become final, I had tried to resolve the past. I'd struggled to figure out the reasons for our dysfunctional marriage and all that had transpired in the last twenty-five years. I had just received the final divorce papers in the mail, and they were dated June 19, 1973. Ron and I were married on June 19, 1948—it was twenty-five years to the day.

I was as upset and confused as an ant whose path to her hill home is blocked by run-off from a heavy rainstorm. My throat tightened up, and tears filled my eyes as I drove to pick up one of the children at school. I still had three of the four kids (all teens) to care for. It was essential that I put on a happy face. My children had endured enough misery and were not responsible in any way.

I had always been a conscientious mother. Now I must be a calm, sober, focused, and cheerful one. In the coming days I moved in a fog of duty, one foot in front of the other. That's the ticket. Don't try to figure it all out right away. Just keep the house clean, feed the family and animals, and go to work. I was very busy selling real estate. I went to choir practice at church and many AA meetings, where they said things like, "Don't think of selling the house or car for a year," and "Take one day at a time," and "Everything will look better soon," and "Don't drink!" I did what I was told, too numb to think, or plan, or decide a single thing for myself. My sweet mother was there for me as she always had been.

During the previous year, while waiting for the divorce to be final, I cried sad tears for the needless loss of a marriage. I did not believe it was a total waste, though, as I had four exceptional children and a grandchild—that was a blessing and I thanked my Higher Power, God, for every moment with them.

It was a Friday night—about two weeks after the divorce was final. I was sitting in the big gold chair in front of the television, trying to concentrate on the program. The house was quiet as all the kids were out with friends. Sam, the black Labrador, and his pal, the yellow cat Caliban, slept by my chair. Suddenly something came over me. I felt this beautiful peace fill my being. A great weight seemed to be lifting from my shoulders. My breathing became solid and deep. My stomach was not in turmoil. I realized at that instant that I was having an exhilarating and illuminating experience. I felt absolutely wonderful. It suddenly hit me. Out loud I yelled, "*I am free!* I do not have to be treated like the maid, or battered, or put down, or made to feel stupid, ugly, and a bad mother ever again."

Yes, I was truly free. I had survived. Twenty-five years. I was whole, healthy, and alive. I felt my entire body wake up. It was a glorious feeling, and at that instant I knew I could face the future with courage, and I was looking forward to it. It was as if I had been released from bondage. I had been unable to live my life as I had wished. I had not been my own boss, my own self, or my own person. Now I was. I owned me! I was on my own. I sat there and sobbed, this time with joy.

I should have done this long ago, but there was no way to change the past. "It took what it took," as we say at the AA Twelve Step meetings. I could not take complete blame for not speaking up to Ron. It had been that way in our era. The majority of men ruled the roost, and most wives minded their husbands.

When I thought back to World War II in the 1940s, it seemed like a million years ago. But that's the way I'd felt back then, hopeful, just barely out of my teens, when our marriage began—when I remembered with a happy heart our falling in love, our beautiful wedding, our apartment, the first house, and motherhood—all those things that I enjoyed in our marriage.

The bad times were quick images of incidents that were intolerable. When I thought of those times, a cold feeling settled into my heart, and I knew I must let go and trust in God. I pushed the suffering down inside me in a search for peace. I did not know at the time that I was experiencing PTSD (Post Traumatic Stress Disorder), that it would last for ten years, or that I was not doing myself any favors. I just couldn't think of the bad times. I had to think of the future. The children would help me with that. They thought only of today and their future. They had dreams too, so I helped them with theirs.

I thought of how my brother, Bob, had landed in France on Omaha Beach, June 6, 1944. He saw so many friends in his unit die that one day. He came home and never spoke of the war until years later, when he was a senior citizen. Thousands of veterans have come home from wars with that disorder. It used to be called "battle fatigue." Ah yes, I too had battle fatigue.

In spite of that, I began to think as I had in my teens. I had a brand new joy for life and many dreams, some new, and some recycled. That's what I must do now. Get my dreams out in the light and live my life as I had wished to before I had married. It wasn't too late. I was only forty-eight years old—I felt young and was gaining self-esteem and confidence. My life was about to start over again.

Think, Speak, Love

Angela Monique Webb-Pigg

He told me....
He told me not to think.
Just don't think about it—he said.
Just let your mind go.

What he wanted was my body,
not my mind.
But how could that be?
They're one in my soul,
connected in me.

But I listened instead,
stopped all thinking in my head.
I chained what once was free
so it could be just him and me.

Next he asked me not speak.
Just listen to me—he said.
I know everything.

What he wanted was my ears
not my voice
But how could this be?
They're also connected in me.

But I listened again,
stopped all speaking in vain.
I let my voice go unsaid
so he would love me instead

Then after a while
after I had long lost my smile
and my actions could not be reconciled,
I forgot who I was.

My voice was gone.
My mind was no longer free.
There was not much left
that was representing me.

I was absent.

See, after he'd got control of me,
took my soul from me,
used my body for his desire
and forced my mind to expire,

he took my words from me,
forced his hurt on me.
I took all the pain
and allowed myself the blame.

I was no more.

With my mind on stop
and my words all ablaze,
it was hard to see through
this lost and lonely phase.

But there was one thing
that he'd failed to seize–
My heart had never stopped its beating.

Even when my mind
had stopped its thinking,
the sound in my heart would never be fleeting.

So when there was nowhere to turn,
when there was no one around,
I looked to my heart
to mend all my broken parts.

Deep down in there
was a love to be found,
a love for myself that

would never be shut down.

I embraced it tightly.
I would never let go.
This love inside me
was mine to have and to hold.

As I held it tighter every day
it pumped blood back in my veins.
It gave strength to my mind
and caused my voice to unwind.

Finally there came the day
I had built up the strength
to use that love for myself
and just walk away.

I walked out on the pain,
my voice and mind regained.
I walked away from the hurt.
I remembered to love myself first.

Night After Court

Janet Vallance

Everyone is in bed
and I am up on stilts and still on
the roller coaster.
And the clown makeup is greasy and smeared.
Wake up.
Call me a cab.
Take me to the mattress store and let us
break the glass and lie on the clean cool foam.
What would I give for the trapeze artist
and lion tamer to take me to tea and read
me a story and count sheep with me until dawn?

Light me a candle.
Bring me some cookies.
I wish all the elephants could keep me warm.
How on earth did cruelty become this possible?
How on earth did the greatest show go so
horribly wrong?

Wake up Lady of the Wire and kiss me goodnight.
Kiss your orphan goodnight.

That Easter

Leonore Wilson

I remember how cold it was that Easter, a bitter cold that kept us in as if it were winter. But the sun was out, a big deception in the sky. We were all at dinner—picture the ham, mashed potatoes, dyed eggs, and jellybeans. Then the phone rang. My mother answered. The dispatcher said people had seen a naked woman running through traffic; she was running like a scared doe in headlights. They couldn't shout her down or weave her in. The dispatcher asked if we had seen her, since she was last spotted running into the open field in back of the house. The police wanted to know if they could come up to the ranch and find her.

A naked girl? Or was it a woman? My mother said it didn't matter and no, we hadn't seen her. Then my husband left the table as if he were a doctor and this was his call. He ran out of the house and so did our boys. I was left with my mother at the table. We were the women. The food, like a big accident, before us. We ate the ham, the salad, drank our milk in silence to the sirens.

My husband came back. He said something about her wearing only underwear, big panties, nothing fancy, and that she had lived in the field for three days. He said she was nothing to look at really. In fact, she looked like a dog, dog ugly. He asked if I would give her a sweatshirt, some pants. I went to the laundry room, picked out the pink ones I hated, the color of peonies. Later I saw her at a distance. They had her handcuffed. They were taking her down the mountain. It was starting to rain.

She had her head down, the way Jesus had his head hung, ready for the crucifixion; she was that scrawny. I put my body in her body. She was wearing my clothes. My husband told me she kept telling the cops that she was a mother, that no mother should be treated with handcuffs, that she was no danger. The cop said she was covered with bruises, that her husband had beaten her and left her on the highway, that she'd wanted to die in the field where she first met him, her lover. The cop said she was on drugs and loony. He said she'd probably go back to her husband. That they always do. These strays, these losers.

That was ten years ago, but I still think of her. This woman, not the only inconsolable stray I've found on my rural road, in this paradise called Napa, this manna of land fluted by canyons, sharpened by cliffs. It's native Wappo territory where wild irises bloom their white flags from the portholes of meadows.

There've been others. Other women. The woman with purple welts around her neck, scourged neck of the black and blue, weeping near her stalled U-Haul and the oversized, drunken tattoo of a man. Or the woman whose husband drove his black sedan behind her as she walked the dotted line, the mean bumper of his souped-up car butting up against her like a bull.

But it was she, the woman discovered on Easter, who remains in my center like the blue throat of the owl in the center of moonlight. She, the vixen's red breath coming out of the garden and into the pitch. She, emerging from the earth-bed like Persephone released from Hades, but returning to Hades. She, the matted camellia, the sodden feathers of the killdeer stirred from the ground. Who is she, whose handiwork? Whose heat did she trigger? What ownership? Who was she, that threadbare girl of skin and ribs, feeling invisible—that field witch?

Did anyone ask her: What are you feeling, do you feel anything, as they cuffed her bare feet, stuffed her in back of that cop car? Was she bound and flogged before he, her lover, her spouse, tossed her out like rotten trash? Is there any way to explain her naked body? Her naked fingers? Her fallen legs collapsing under her like unplayed cards?

I think of her, of all the women I have found in my rural country, their shadows writhe within me. I, who have stayed silent. They with their loosened hair, stained with soil and blood, drugged eyes glazed forever on the black chart of amnesia. There have been many in these hills, this valley. Wild, hard women. Endangered sisters. Their heaped colors suddenly gone ashen like the cloudiness that forms over winter blacktop. They, who scratch themselves, who urinate, who stay in unspeakable loneliness; their feminine power routed backward like miles of barbwire. They are homeless, cursed women, naughty women, their words stolen out of their teeth like bread. They, who would rather choke than be vulgar.

How can I wrap my house in sleep thinking of them, thinking of her making a fire of wet wood, telling stories to herself, singing lullabies, nursing the tragedy of her sex. I pace the floor thinking of her. I poke my spade into the dry loam and think of her. I find her everywhere. I have learned her by heart. I have worn her close to my body. For she is my body. She is the foundling of the woods, the one slip of tongue, the liquid mist that burns off the highway as the new day forms.

I want to know who touched the match to her flesh, who left her blanketless in the frost as I stoked and blazed my stove. I know she was there in the twilight and thorns. I've felt her mouth on mine like a lump of bitter jelly all those times alcohol was fire on my breath. The times I starved myself with pills in my pocket, wanting love, wanting the brisk taste of airports and ferries, I've been her. The times I wanted the impermissible. I've been her.

Discontent as a cormorant that pokes around the corpses of roses, wanting to be fractured, exiled under the floss of many petals, I've been her. Wanting to be seduced by that floral nard. Me, in the snowstorm of unimaginable longing, while the hangman's noose tightened inside my chest, taunting, taunting. I, too, tried on death too many times. I, who wore my own bruises like badges around my jaw. I, of steely posture.

Why?

I lowered myself in the chaparral, afraid, my breasts full of milk, my hair disheveled. I thought I could stand betrayal, that I could spill myself like purple vetch, like legend down the lush game trails into drink. What soothed me? Sometimes mint in the mouth, sometimes the pearl-gray mist. I wanted to be like my ancestors. I wanted to be strong as shattered rock, as basalt mortars. I didn't think it right that a woman go off like a kettle full boil. But I was proud and half-blind. I was a stuttering tadpole. A spectacle. An odd, empty thing.

I was a master of nothing. I wrestled with the serpent inside me, the female totem of melancholy. Me, with my teacups and miniature cakes. I sucked in my midnights, my howls and my whelps. Why? How many dead girls like me smelled of old lunatic lies? My sentence was mine: my well-piped breeding, my pilgrim dreams. Guardian of chandeliers, when my heart was always squawking like an interior swan.

Be damned the well-scrubbed house, the family snapshots. Be damned the flowers of Hell, the ostracized penance, the lowermost regions, Lethe's spell where Eurydice wastes away with Persephone. Be damned if the dark snake of Eden flew out of my mouth. I want the Easter woman at my table, I want her story. I want to take her groggy hand, lead her away from the fettered ring, the life of sacrifice, of thick-scented curses. My tongue dips into the chewed meat of thistled honey when I say this.

Mothering is the dilation of feathers. Forget the flower-pressed face concealing its failures, bleeding its kindness like a parasite. Inside our smile is the knife-grind, the winged lion. What abscesses in our flesh—not our humiliation, nor our quarrel, but our rising.

Noon

"...she takes up what she has found / and runs! /
She is bringing it back, brave girl! //
And with her own bright hatchet / she chops chops chops /
through the roaring and the sky // shuddering /
she chops chops chops // she keeps on chopping"

—Ruth Thompson, "Jill and the Beanstalk," *Woman with Crows*

An Open Letter to Rihanna from Lilith
Jaz Sufi

Rihanna—

Adam and I, we were born like a single chord,
the syncing of our heartbeats the world's first duet,
spotlights bursting from our throats.

Man may have been made in God's image,
                but woman was made in mine.
Eve was only a cover song—
she was the sampling of a single verse and not the chorus,
a radio edit to soften sharp edges, safe and stupid
                and simple to swallow.

Call Genesis the first Autotune.

I came first, though,
before Adam had the excuse of a missing rib—
and, Rihanna,
I know that with men who walk like hit singles,
                there are always excuses.
Yours says he watched his mother's husband beat her bloody,
like how Adam watched our Father force
                the very earth into being with his fists.

These men expect their women
                to be back-up singers, to harmonize
with their spotlight solos, to keep dissent muted in our chests
like a broken microphone. We are the choir,
                meant to wait for them
to write our lyrics, do not sing unless spoken to,
we are best when we are quavering vibrato
                not blowing out speakers.

One day, he tried to push me to lay on my back beneath him.

I pushed back.

Eden was not worth this—swallowing my self-respect
to lie with my dignity in the dust beneath him.
The tabloids, the album sales,
they aren't worth the black eyes and bruises.
Your dignity is not a price tag.
Your heart is not an album on clearance.
Us women are not record stores
waiting to be looted by greedy hands.

God sent angels to bring me back, and
              their words were just radio static.
I was the record scratch to God's concerto,
and my only regret is not shredding the sheet music behind me.

Fuck the duets—if God will not give us music,
we can sing a capella. Let our heartbeats be the bass.
If the newspapers call you demon,
let every church you pass burn.

If you need an example of what it is to stand alone on a stage,
let me be your example, because you, too, are an example.
There are daughters of Eve watching
every step you take back to him,
lip-synching along to every time you stay silent.

The gates of Eden clanged shut like a funeral dirge behind me,
and I did not look back. There was no second time.
Don't let there be a second time,
Rihanna, daughter, you are better than this.

Stop smiling for the cameras.

Get off your back,

and go.

Blood and Fire

Christy Hoss

Town gossips were wrong about Gabriel.

Abbey determined to make tonight's celebration a success to prove it. The aroma of garlic bread and lasagna baking battled for dominance over the musty odor of the two-room basement apartment. No matter if the flatware didn't match and the plates were different sizes; newlyweds had to start somewhere.

This will prove I know what he's needed from a woman. Stability.

A shadow passed the rectangular window next to the bottom of the flat's single entrance. Abbey skipped stairs to the top landing, ready to plant a sultry kiss on the man of her dreams. She swallowed hard and held her breath, wishing.

Keys jingled and the knob turned. Gabriel forced the door, smacking Abbey into the flimsy handrail. His heavy stomps made the old wooden steps creak. Abbey rubbed the small of her back and followed.

His spirit will pick up after he eats.

Plopping on the couch, Gabriel leaned back and ran his hands through his salt and pepper hair. Abbey approached him from behind the couch and slid her arms around his neck, kissing his salty ear. She thought she sensed his smile and read it as an invitation to move further to kiss his neck on her way to his lips, but he grabbed her wrist, squeezing until his knuckles turned white. Abbey yelped in pain.

"Did I hurt you?"

She backed away, rubbing a red hand mark circling her wrist. The garlic smell of lasagna, ready to be eaten, interrupted her thoughts, and she remembered the evening's quest.

"I made you a special dinner." She rounded the corner of the couch and knelt by his side. "It's our fifth month anniversary. Don't you want to celebrate?" She rested her head on his lap, hoping his eyes would meet her passionate gaze. He continued to stare ahead, unmoved by her offering. She closed her eyes.

His hand ruffled the back of her dress as it moved upward. She waited for a caress. He gripped the neatly brushed French knot and yanked her head back, breaking her barrette; its pieces skittered in all directions. Abbey winced at his strength.

"Gabe," she asked, "what are you doing?"

He released his grip and resumed his lifeless stare into nothingness. Abbey stood. A tear dripped down her cheek. The caution flag waved. Friends had warned her, but she'd casually excused his dominating behavior. She was his hope, his savior, one who would renew his life. Gathering the broken pieces, she slunk into the kitchen and fed the trash.

Hot breath blew on her neck, and her skin rippled with goose bumps. Gabriel whipped her around, squeezing her shoulders as if trying to fold her in half. "Didn't you think I would figure it out? I'm not an idiot, you know." Angry spittle spattered in her face.

"I have no idea what you're talking about." Her knees wobbled like Jell-O dropped from out of a mold.

Gabriel let go, stomped to the dresser and pawed around in her top drawer. Abbey gingerly approached as he turned to face her, holding the object of his rage. "I found this when I came home for lunch today." He held out a ceramic frame laced with tiny roses; in its center was a photo of Abbey hugging an old beau.

Abbey's heart sunk to her toes. It hadn't been that long since she had made her choice. Fond memories, still fresh from her recent experience, had not allowed her to forget them completely, and she had hidden the photo. Apparently not well enough.

"We haven't been settled long enough for me to sort things out. It's an old photo. It's nothing."

"Liar!"

His fierceness caused Abbey to step backward into the kitchen. Stumbling against the table, a carafe of ice water toppled, splattering the floor. Gabriel approached, clutching the frame, profanities spewing from his mouth.

"You're my wife, not his. This should have been trashed before you took my ring!"

The timer buzzed. The lasagna was done.

"I'm sorry," she whimpered.

He smacked the frame on the cement, sending glass shards scattering across the floor. The photo landed in the spilled water. His foot stomped and twisted to mangle the image of the competition. "I should have known you were a whore when we first met." He gripped her arm and twisted it behind her back. She screamed.

"Stop it, Gabriel, you're hurting me." Her cries reached to the support beams of the house above.

The timer continued to buzz.

Shoving her toward the couch, he pushed her over its back side. Her thin frame somersaulted over the couch, landing her feet on the floor. Dizzied by the sudden flip, she lay stunned. Gabriel dropped on her, clawing and tossing her on the couch, a lion preying on a lame gazelle. Fist after fist pummeled her skull, accompanied with female-degrading profanities.

"I'm going to kill you! You goddamn bitch!"

BUZZZZ…

Abbey flung her hands to her temples in defense. She had to get away, run for help, but the only way out was up the stairs, and Gabriel blocked her escape. She was going to die. But she didn't want to, not in a basement before her twentieth birthday.

BUZZZZ…

"Help me! Help me!" Terror screamed from her lungs, and Gabriel continued to beat her head as she sunk deeper and deeper into the sagging couch. *Doesn't anyone hear me?* Blackness and a million spinning stars hazed her vision. Strength faded from her limbs.

I don't want to die.

From deep in her gut a flicker of hope sparked, kindling the desire to live and fight for survival.

I was meant for more than this.

Cowering from the blows, she mustered one last yelp. "God help me!"

The Almighty heard her plea, as angels seemed to whisk her to her feet, up the steps and out the door.

No Rights

Juanita J. Martin

Imprisoned our bodies,
held our tongues—
We became victims along with our children
with no protection from the courts.

Society closed its eyes like the justice system
while the brutality continued upon us.
We became slaves with no rights,
whipped with insults as well as fists.

We're not waiting for laws to evolve
while living on the edge of fear and shame.
Every fourth woman takes a stand—
We are no longer silent.

Familiar Click

Madeleine Keegan O'Connell

He locked the door and she heard a familiar click,
knowing what was to come.
The abuse came regularly now,
and she had become numb.

The next day she saw the hand that struck her
raised against her child.
With that one blow the time had come
for the number she would dial.

The changes which were so long in coming
now seemed to move so fast.
Overnight her escape became real
and there was no turning back.

Today she locks the door herself
and hears a familiar click.
She may not know what is to come,
but she's quite clear what will not.

Loose Change
Dani Burlison

She hadn't left the confines of her house in days. Not even to retrieve her mail or refill the bird feeder, which hung like a shriveling pear from the front porch's awning. Her faithful gray cat, Leo, kept her tethered, distracted. She felt like Leo's spindle of thread, slowly unraveling at first, and then gaining momentum, while everything she knew piled up like those knots of ivory thread around her.

She had gathered loose change from the dresser, throwing the coins into a Ziploc bag. Now she fondled them nervously inside her pocket. She pinched the individual coins through the plastic encasement, identifying each as either a dime, nickel, or penny. Bead-sized lint balls and bent safety pins pressed against her thigh. This day, most of the coins were pennies. One was a fifty-cent Euro she held onto for good luck during travels.

Her wallet welcomed her weathered hands and revealed an envelope of one-hundred-dollar bills. *One, two, three, four, five.* More than enough to take a bus to San Diego and catch another to La Paz. Or enough to get a one-way ticket north, maybe to the cold, vast stretch of Saskatchewan. *Anywhere but here.*

Too many cups of milky black tea, with too many teaspoons of white sugar, kept her on edge, as if she needed to hide or run. Or just fade away. The time had come to fade away, to go.

She had been a fixture in his life; a cabinet door, a windowsill. Something he expected to be there, still and ignored, a receptacle for all of the things he didn't want to hold: anger, frustration, loathing. He unloaded those onto her like a wrecking ball.

She had turned inside out, a self-destructing star, a collapsed nebula, disappearing at light speed.

Today, she found herself leaving. She gathered her pennies and clothes from the dryer and headed for the bus station. The tattered screen door smacked behind her. She spared one glance back for Leo who looked startled, confused.

She put one foot in front of the next, her pace quickening. Shallow breath growing deeper, louder as the pavement disappeared behind her heels, backpack banging out a rhythm against her spine. Faster, running, flying. She was off, unlatched, free; the fifty-cent Euro clutched in her hand.

Even a Woman
Michelle Wing

Every day I ran.

The dog and I alone on a hiking trail,
middle of the day, only our panting breath
and footsteps to break the silence. Although
she was not there, I ran from the nightmares,

away from shadows, tried to calm
the startle reflex that tightened
each muscle of my hunted body, quivering
until exhaustion gave me stillness

enough to return to the little cabin
in the woods where no one knew
how to find me. I was in hiding,
one of the disappeared. New town,

unlisted phone number, quit the job
I used to have because I could not afford
to leave any trace. I had shrunk into
that victim role, the one abandoned

so long ago. This caught me off guard,
unprepared. My running shoes tossed
to the back of the closet. Weren't these
days locked in my past? I didn't know

a woman could be the bad guy too.
After months of bullying, tantrums
and road rage, a crumbling beneath
her harsh words and jealousies,

I found enough courage to leave.
And then the stalking began, a
car outside my apartment at night,

assaults at the gym, letters sent

to my boss, harassing phone calls,
the restraining order claiming I was
the one on the brink of insanity.
I came to court, hoping for justice.

The judge dismissed all charges.

My girlfriend weighed 115 pounds,
stood five feet, four inches tall.
They were all thinking, "What is she afraid of?"

But even a woman can make you run.

Battered

Ana Manwaring

The gray sycamores lining Broadway shiver in the sleet that angles sharply through them to the ground. A brief sunset stains the storm clouds a bruised, purple-black like the days-old shiner I wear under my carefully-applied makeup. I squint through the windshield against the garish glare cast on the wet pavement by headlights. Darkness settles down on the city, and neither the glow of street lamps, nor the distant lights of the city center shrouded in mist lift the heaviness. There are few people about, and those scurry for shelter, bundled in rain gear. My radio sounds scratchy, like an old phonograph record.

The boulevard widens and here Broadway is tree-lined and dotted by grand homes on large, manicured lots. I have come from farther north, a place of narrow streets, untamed landscaping and small houses. Some are in disrepair, their cracked paint peeling, windows broken, and screens hanging loose.

The mansions give way to modern commercial buildings as I drive through downtown. From an overpass, I see that parts of the city are dark, the electricity blown out like cheap bar matches. That's why I'm in my car, buffeted by a storm on this winter's eve. I've been blown out.

I grip my steering wheel until my unhurt hand aches. The streets are eerie-calm and dark. The radio's static, louder here, grates my muscles. I punch it off. South Broadway is derelict and looks mean. The gutters and storm drains overflow. Churning brown, the foul water collects in low spots on the road. Trash submerges in this gutter stew. My headlights catch the face of misery in a doorway, then all is black along the graffiti-crusted brick of the tenements, liquor stores and cheap rent-by-the-hour hotels. Mine is the only car moving. I think, *I hope he hasn't followed me*.

Lightning slashes across every garbage bin and sodden cat, suspending them against a littered alley in slow motion, the way his fist smashed through the brittle screen of our domestic content. I swerve with the boom of thunder that follows and nearly crash. Images of the orange alley cats and green dumpsters shift orange to purple, green to red in my eyes. More angry thunder wallops the night. I feel the impact through the metal frame of my car. My bones ache.

I turn off South Broadway into a dark neighborhood of low bungalows as the thunderstorm slows its fury. I make several turns, pull into an alley, shut off the engine, turn out my lights and wait. I go numb with the waiting. Is it cold in the car? I restart the engine and dial the heat to "HIGH," but it's useless—my body shivers and quakes in tempo with my anger. Still, I idle behind the dumpsters in this alley until I am certain he hasn't followed, then race through the steady downpour toward my destination. It takes several minutes to leave this working-class neighborhood, double back to the boulevard, and cross the southern part of the city to another district.

I stop in front of a large house. The electricity is restored here and the rain has slacked to a misty drizzle. I have come a dozen times before with my suitcase, my pounding head, and my throbbing bruises. As before, I sit in my car across from the shelter. I watch the house through the mist and my own tears. My wrist shrieks with searing pain—is it broken?

The tops of women's heads pass back and forth past a small, high window that does not have the curtain drawn. "Perhaps it's a kitchen," I say aloud, confused by the thickness of my unfamiliar voice. My tongue fills my mouth and I feel sharp scraping against it. Has he broken a tooth? I try to swallow, but my throat is dry. I'm certain there will be cool water in that kitchen, and I'm comforted by the thought. My muscles relax slightly.

I start to open the car door, but my body has stiffened and I have trouble moving. The pain stabs through my shoulder when I push against the door, but the beacon of women shining from the window strengthens me. I push the door with new determination. It swings open and I fall to the wet pavement and rest there until the sickening pain recedes to an ache, and I haul myself up, using the car as a crutch. When I am standing, I reach for my handbag, close the door, and limp across the street into the yard. Comforting sounds of cooking and television waft through the small window.

It is agony to mount the steps to the porch. I drag my battered body up one step and then another. White spots pop and glow before my eyes; I need to put my head down. But there are only a few steps more. *It will be safe inside,* I tell myself.

I raise my hand to knock and hear a rustling along the box hedge lining the walkway. Help is coming. I half turn to the sound.

"Help," my sluggish tongue pleads, "Help me, please!"

A bundled–up figure emerges from the darkness and steps heavily onto the wooden stair.

A hand reaches out, steadies me. "Hello, darling. I've been waiting for you."

Unlost and Unforgotten

Spirette Dotter

heart beating wildly, I gasp
at the center of an intersection
red light, traffic paused,
the click-clicking of my turn signal
marks every crucial moment—
our destiny hangs on a fleeting prayer

wide-eyed, I search for escape
as shrilling sirens speed closer toward us
blaring bullhorns sound
like sledgehammers thrashing in my head
slapped by truth of the moment—
I realize life, as we know it, will end

they found us, I am certain
my insides flip upside down, rise slowly,
then lodge in my throat
while blue and red lights flash behind me
trapped in terror this moment—
I wait, haunted, as they come to take me

surrendering, I tremble
just don't place my babies with him!
I plead, in my mind,
wishing we'd be lost, hidden, forgotten,
together, safe, each moment—
instead—we're unlost, and unforgotten

Fight-or-Flight Impaired

Spirette Dotter

Shallow breath suspended
eyes widened in terror
my rapid pulse triggering
a frenzied, anguished rush—
Yet…I sit stiff, unmoving, tears frozen
the moment etched in a vacuum of time

"I *will* kill them!" he yells
throwing clothes in a bag
"You'll never see them again!"
The babies howl, "Mama!"
Still…silently screaming, I hold them tight
No safe place to turn to, nowhere to run

We make it through the night
then flee while he's at work
Months later, I stand in a courtroom
proof of abuse in hand—
Yet…alone, nauseous, and trembling in fear
I hear the judge grant *him* sole custody

Shallow breath suspended
eyes widened in terror
my rapid pulse triggering
a frenzied, anguished rush—
Still…I stand stiff, unmoving, tears frozen
the moment etched in a vacuum of time

Tainted Vows

Renelaine Pfister

For better or for worse, for richer or for poorer, in sickness and in health, till death do us part. Marriage. It's the aim of so many people. To some, they don't have real lives unless they find a partner and marry that person. They orchestrate their whole lives around the institution of marriage. But for people like him, it's nothing but a mistake.

He first saw her on vacation in Costa Rica. She was walking on the beach, wearing a colorful sarong, her red hair streaming behind her. He thought she was gorgeous. Love at first sight and all of that. Only later did he learn that she hated the beach. She didn't even like going to Costa Rica; she despised traveling. The packing, the organizing, living in a strange place and listening to a foreign language; none of it appealed to her.

She was forced to go to Costa Rica by her childhood girl-friend, who was dating a man who lived there. Her girlfriend had met the man on the Internet and this was their first meeting. She'd dragged Simone to make sure the man wasn't a rapist or a creep, and when her friend was satisfied, she'd ditched her and now she was alone, walking on the beach, because she didn't know what else she should do. Their hotel was within walking distance.

He saw her walking and he fell in love. Wasn't it always that simple? He approached her, and she smiled at him. He gave up his life in Rhode Island for her and moved to Oregon to be with her. But it was all worth it, because she adored him. They went for hikes and long drives, cooked together, and made love. Coffee, and movies, and showers together. Their life was blissful.

It lasted a year. That was the extent of their romance as a married couple. After that, things shifted. It was as if Simone went to bed one night and another woman rose out of it. Kafka's *Meta-morphosis* was nothing compared to the change in her. At least the bug was still Gregor Samsa on the inside. But Simone was changed inside and out. She suddenly stopped caring about her appearance. She didn't put on makeup. She left her hair un-combed. Her clothes didn't match.

He didn't mind the physical change as much as he did her behavior. She suddenly became irritable and short-tempered. She snapped at him over minor things. She disagreed with him over everything. He couldn't do or say anything right. Every time she looked at him, she seemed disgusted by him. And she refused his touch. But she touched him in a different way.

The first time she hit him, he thought it was just a joke. He'd kidded about something, and she'd swatted his arm, which didn't hurt. He'd laughed, and she hit his arm harder. The next time, when they had an argument, she picked up his cell phone and threw it at him. It left a bruise on his chest. He was more surprised than anything else. But she grew progressively worse. Realizing that her hands didn't carry much clout on him, she used a football, a frying pan, and a chair to throw at him when she got angry with him.

For better or for worse, for richer or for poorer, in sickness and in health, till death do us part.

Now it was only for worse. Never for better.

A bruise on his thigh where she'd hit him with a baseball bat looked black and yellow, like an old banana. Scratches on his arms where she'd dragged her fingernails left red trails that his co-workers wondered at. He always had an excuse ready. He should say something, but how could he? He felt ashamed and less than a man. Who would even believe him? Who would believe that he, six feet tall and a hundred ninety pounds, got attacked by a woman five feet four and a hundred and thirty pounds?

This last time, he had accidentally hit her in the face when he shook his arm free, and he knocked her down. She was lying there, unmoving. His red-haired demon, momentarily at peace. The baseball bat, which was now her favorite weapon, clattered a few inches away from her hands.

Till death do us part.

He saw she was beginning to stir and quickly picked up the baseball bat. He took it with him when he left the house—forever.

Thank You, Mama!
Dianna L. Grayer

Tears roll down my face
remembering the pain of
my parents' struggle to communicate.

Unable to speak the language of their minds,
of their hearts,
of their souls.
Their truths camouflaged.
Their needs and desires restrained.
Their essences distorted.
Their spirits unseen.

Intimate moments were a constant roar.
Bullets of disdain.
Threats and humiliation.
A destructive system, stabilized in chaos.

The only option for peace
to run away.
My mother a runaway!

Thank you, Mama.
Thank you, Mama,
for knowing,
for trusting Spirit,
for saving me!

Mama, I've learned.
After many years of witnessing
I've learned by watching the incessant pouring of pain.
Mama, I've learned what not to do.

Mama, I'm sorry for your hurt,
your struggle.
It lives in me.

Your light unseen.
Your wounding masked by thunderous rage.
I'm sorry, Mama.

Mama, I had to learn
what I witnessed affected me.
I clammed up. I retreated into my shell.
My true self-bound and guarded.
I had to learn to set free my essence.
Reveal my light.
Honor my soul.
Respect my wisdom.

But guess what, Mama?
The skills you lacked,
the skills I lacked and
the skills the ones before you lacked.
This cycle has stopped! Copuff! Finished!

Mama, I vowed not to be subjected to negativity.
No one would hurt me and I would hurt no one.
Mama, I've learned to express from my heart—not my reactions.
With trial and error, I never lost hope.
I have learned.

Mama, I've learned.
After many years of witnessing,
I've learned by my watching the incessant pouring of pain.
Mama, I've learned what not to do.

I've learned to be myself.
Fierce and smart and loving and creative,
no longer hidden within my shell,
no longer distrusting and passive.
No longer unimportant.

Thank you, Mama, for saying enough is enough.
Thank you for planting the seed.
The seed that told me I—could—leave.
The seed of my worthiness.

Thank you, Mama!
For leaving.
For planting a garden of opportunity.
For saving yourself and
saving me.

Thank you, Mama!

Fragments
Barbara Kephart Immel

One of my earliest memories is the warmth of Mom's body. She holds me while we both nap on the couch. She is behind me, with her arm protectively across my waist to keep me from falling. I feel warm and loved and safe.

It's summertime. Country music blares on the radio. I follow the sound to the kitchen. Mom washes the floor on hands and knees, weeping. Mommy, what's wrong? Nothing, honey, go out and play. Tears run down her face onto the floor, right before she wipes them away with a sponge. Mommy, what's wrong? Nothing, honey. I want you to go outside and play.

I hear scary sounds at night from Mom and Dad's bedroom. I am too scared to leave bed.

Mom takes us to the park after school. I start going down the slide. My baby sister with her soft, brown curls has her back to me and is not getting off the slide. I pitch off the slide instead of hitting her in the back and hurt my arms really badly. Mom calls Dad, but he stays at work and insists on having dinner before taking me to the hospital. I lie on the couch. Mom tries to coax me to eat corn, my favorite, but I'm not hungry. When we get to the hospital, I get a shot. Later a nice man gently feels both arms. Someone puts a mask over my face. The nice man quickly sets the bone, and I suck in gas in pain.

I listen in the hallway every day for the slightest sound of Mom and Dad having a fight. Sundays are the worst. He's home all day on Sundays.

Dad chases Mom around the house with a butcher knife. He rips the coffeepot she just bought from the wall and hurls it to the floor, splashing hot coffee everywhere. He threatens to kill her, chop her into little pieces, and feed her to the sharks.

Mom comes home after a week in the hospital for back surgery. My sisters are twelve and nine and I'm almost fourteen. Dad drives Grandmother to the Greyhound station because he doesn't want her around. Once home, he tries to get Mom up. I tell him she's not supposed to. He becomes enraged and fights me. I try to call the police, but he throws a heavy captain's chair at me. I duck, and the chair hits the wall, splintering into pieces. Mom gets up later and hides the splinters in the garage.

The next day, my sisters and I are in the garage. Dad comes in, sees the splinters and asks what happened to my chair? My youngest sister says, "You threw it at Bobbie. Don't you remember?" He doesn't, and returns to the house. I summon my courage and go back into the house to make sure Mom is OK.

He keeps pulling at her to get her up. He will not leave her alone. I jump on his back to stop him, wailing on him with my fists. He backs me up into the wall, hard. I hit spine first, fall to the floor and get back up fighting.

He is furious with my baby sister. He chases her into her bedroom. She scurries under the bed. He rips the bed up and over her head, as she cries and rolls back and forth to get back to safety under the bed.

Four of us hide in the laundry room near the only other exit from the house. He leaves. I call my uncles and ask them to please come get us or he is going to kill us. It's a five-hour drive for them. We flee with nothing, arriving in Mom's hometown in the wee hours of August 31, 1970.

What I have learned is that getting help to leave safely is critical. We were able to stay with family. (The first woman's shelter didn't open in the United States until the mid-1970s.) The good news is that there are so many more resources available now, including 911 and reaching out to hot lines and shelters such as the YWCA, or to your doctor or clinic. I also learned to trust my instincts, and to have courage. Only the women involved know when they're truly in danger, and the situation has become untenable. We fled when Mom could no longer protect herself or us girls, and I could not protect us.

Mom used to say a bad dad is better than no dad at all. (Her father died in a ranch accident during the Great Depression.) Looking back, I disagree. No one deserves to be abused or to witness abuse of people they love, or to suffer the lifelong psychological and physical damage abuse causes to the person being abused and their children, no matter how young they are when they witness the abuse. Depression, anyone? Heart disease, stroke, or other serious illnesses, including a possibly shorter lifespan?

How'd we all do? We immediately went on welfare, a divine safety net. My aunts and uncles got us set up in a duplex with gently used beds, pots and pans, and linens. Mom returned to work after recovering from surgery, and she divorced my father. She supported the four of us until we were able to start lives of our own, and lived twenty-seven years free of Dad, surrounded by friends and family. She wanted all of us girls to study hard and go to college, and we did. I am in awe of what Mom did, escaping when she was incapacitated, and being a single parent and supporting three daughters completely on her own.

If I could have a redo, I would report the abuse earlier and/or encourage and help Mom to leave sooner. We survived because we escaped to a safe place with the help of God and other people. We made it. And so can you.

Rebecca's Slippers

Kate Farrell

No more arguments. She bit her fingernails. Nothing she'd ever said had stopped him before. This time she was ready.

Tonight she'd waited up, not daring to sleep since he was out later than usual. That meant only one thing: He would be a raging drunk. She wore her warm, fleece bathrobe and fleece-lined moccasin slippers with rubber soles, prepared to flee if necessary. A position in the downstairs hallway was best, she thought, near the kitchen and its back door. When his car came careening down their steep driveway, she scurried to the kitchen, thinking she could pretend to be making a cup of tea.

"'Becca! Where are you? I've been trying to call you all night!" He stalked towards their bedroom on the upper level.

"Rob! I'm down here, in the kitchen."

"So, you're just getting in? Where've you been?" He yelled to her while stomping down the stairs.

"Oh, no, hon. I've been home all evening. Just couldn't sleep."

"How could you be home when I've been trying to call you and no answer?" He glared at her from over the railing.

Rebecca took the exact position she'd staked out, holding the teacup, with her back to the wall next to the kitchen door. "I've been here all night, watching late shows. Are you sure you called the right number?"

"What do you mean, 'Did I call the right number?' I know my own damn phone number. Now, where were you?" He strode down the hallway and put both hands on the wall, one on either side of her. His face was inches away, smelling of sour whiskey.

She was not going to stand there and let him hit her. Never again. Rebecca dropped to her knees, sending the teacup rolling across the floor—crawled, stumbled, ran through the kitchen and out the back door, slamming it. Her anxiety propelled her up the steep hill between the houses; she slipped in the loose dirt, clawed at shrubs, grabbed at tree limbs, then gained traction. She heard Rob shout, crash down the backstairs, curse.

When she reached the paved street, she ran—down to the

end of the block and to the footpath that continued up the hill in this upscale neighborhood of homes with decks and picture windows that looked out to the twinkling lights of the city far below. Hidden from streetlights in the shadowy lane, she slowed slightly, breathless. Noises from nearby houses floated through the night air: music, laughter, barking dogs. She couldn't stop, listened only for footsteps, and quickened her pace to reach higher ground.

At the white trail sign that marked the entrance to a jogging path along the flat rim of the hilltop, she finally rested. Looking up to the stars, she felt the first glimmer of hope. Her plan was to wait him out in this isolated spot and when it was light, find help. It would only be a few more hours. She settled down in a bower of pine needles and leaned against a rock, her heart still racing.

A rustling noise startled her. Was it footsteps? She heard someone or something coming through the brush. She stood up, looking for a way out, then tripped and fell hard to the ground. She panicked, feeling the earth tremble and then split open. Her body slipped through the crack and spiraled downward for a long, long way.

She came to an abrupt stop, landing on a spongy, damp surface, remarkably unharmed. She felt mud and opened her eyes. She was sitting in a marsh, near a sluggish, brown stream in a vast cavern, lit only by torches set in the walls. Where was she and how could she get out?

Her body was poised for flight, so she ran, plunging headlong into an unknown, uneven terrain. Hearing a horrifying growl ahead, she instinctively diverted her path into a side cavern. If only she'd thought to bring some water. She looked frantically around and almost screamed.

There, in the deepest corner, were three ancient women with threads. Somehow, Rebecca knew them. Could it be real? Was she hallucinating? Had she suffered a concussion?

"We can see you, even if you think we're not real," said the youngest of the three women, while spinning a thread from her hand-held distaff, down to the ever-turning spindle. Her long, dark hair was disheveled, her gown tattered and soiled. Yet her fingers never stopped moving and guided the thread like a spider's legs, nimble and swift.

"You're not! You are. The Fates of Moirae." Rebecca drew closer. Even in her dread, her curiosity was piqued. How confused she'd been all her life. She'd asked for help from fortunetellers who read palms and Tarot cards, seeking her way. Here in this gloomy place, she might know the truth at last.

"Don't take another step," said Lachesis, the middle one who pulled the thread from the spindle. "You don't want to get tangled in this life line or break it." She continued to pull a single thread and measure its length, careful not to fray its strands.

"I'm always getting into fixes, tangles, and I don't know why." Rebecca said.

"Do you know the meaning of your own name?" Clotho asked, the first sister with dark eyes that flitted from her spinning work to Rebecca and back again. "Names are no accident, not ever."

"It's a family name, traditional, old fashioned," she answered.

"It means snare," said the third Fate, Atropos. "It means a knotted cord, from the ancient days. You are quite a silly girl, falling into your own traps."

"No one in my family ever told me my name meant that. How ugly." Rebecca sighed and all the air in her seemed to dissipate. She sank to the rocky soil, held her head in her hands, and wept. She was in the worse snare of all. She heard the snip, snip of cruel Atropos, cutting the thread, fixing the time of death for one human after the other.

"You came here for an answer, didn't you? Running away, aren't you?" Atropos asked, pointing her sharp scissors at Rebecca. "Clotho may know your birth destiny, but what have you done to fulfill it?"

"How can I fulfill what I don't know?" Rebecca began wailing in earnest at the Fates. "Why are you so hidden, secreted away, remote from all we do?

"We are always near," said Clotho. "Don't you feel the breeze from the upper world? It wafts back and forth as a wind. It speaks to the trees and the trees sigh to the birds. All the Earth is filled with the truth about life, every life. Haven't you heard?" Her eyes filled with a sudden joy.

"I never heard a thing about my life." Rebecca realized she was flirting with Fate, acting like a sullen child. She paused, and in that moment she could remember hearing the wind, its soft touch, its song. She opened her hands and knew. "I hold on too tight. I think I need people and won't let them go, even when it's long past time to let go. I think I need lots of things. But, look. I'm here. I've let go of everything. Here with my messy robe, granny gown, and slippers." She looked up and saw a glint in the eyes of all three Fates and thought that was a good sign.

She took a deep breath, feeling the rightfulness of her own truth. "I'm here to help others see the traps in their lives, where they get stuck and tangled. I've been tangled up enough to know." A vision came to her, talking to a group of people, counseling them with passion, untying their knots. She stood up and brushed the dried mud from her robe.

"Now I see my path ahead. How do I get out of here?" Rebecca asked. She looked around as if for the first time, at the dank cavern of the Underworld. Had she been that close to death? Shivering, she knew that, too.

"I'd follow the sound of the dog," said Clotho. "It's the only way out."

"Thank you. I owe you my life."

"We know," they said as one voice.

Heartened, she returned to the open space where the roof of the great grotto was lost high in the shadows. The sharp barks of what must be a gigantic dog echoed throughout the chamber. As she drew near, she saw the monster was not so enormous; it was just that he had three heads, all barking at once. Picking up loose rocks, she threw them in one direction, then another. The dog's heads snarled at each one, back and forth, in confusion. Rebecca slipped through his legs into a splendid palace beyond: the home of the shades and their queen, Persephone.

"Ah, my dear Rebecca, you've arrived just in time for the dance." Persephone spoke to her from a raised platform. Her long, black gown swirled with jewels, her dark hair bound with a bright crown of rubies. At her word, the hoop drummer began a steady rhythm, then quickened his beat; the flutist sang out with a long, yearning call, and the lyre struck up a joyful tune. From out of the depths the skeletons rose and joined hands. They knew it by heart—*la danse macabre*, the dance of death.

"What a rousing tune!" Rebecca reached into the circle of line dancers and kicked up her heels to the clacking of the dancers' bones. She felt she could dance forever, free and fearless, with the defying courage of the dead.

"Come to me, Rebecca." The queen called to her, gesturing gracefully to join her on the dais. Rebecca stepped up and gazed into the deep, black pools that were the queen's eyes and knew no more.

It was the sunshine on her face that woke her. Rebecca stretched and tried to get up, but every bone and muscle ached. She groaned.

"Did you hear something over there?" A woman asked her husband on the jogging path.

"I see something moving," her husband answered, walking over.

"Oh no! What's happened to you?" The woman found Rebecca lying on the ground in a tattered, filthy robe. "Are you hurt? Do you need a doctor?"

"I'm fine now. I ran away. Do you have any water?" As the woman fussed over her, Rebecca looked at her clothes. She wasn't really certain what had happened. But one thing she could not ignore. The soles of her new slippers were completely worn out.

Bearing Witness

Kalia Mussetter

Help begins with bearing witness,
so I am watching her with great care.
I am watching her struggle, yet again.
I am watching her under his boot.
I am watching his boot stomp her,
      first with broken glass and mud,
then very soon after, with velvet and roses:
the sole of him on her changes, hard to soft, but it's still his boot.
I am watching her bruise; the place where she has just been hit
again.
I am watching her photograph this purple-brown island floating
deep-rooted on the muscle of her thigh
in hopes that she is making a map
that policemen and lawyers and judges can follow,
      as if by breadcrumbs,
to lead her out, finally,
to safety
away from him.
I am watching, with joy, her laughing with her daughters,
these two young women she has given to the world, bringing
all her beauty with them.
I am watching her sing, and make everything
      OK with him in public.
I am watching her being belittled by him in public.
I am watching this once again,
the most recent time of many, many times.
I am watching inside as anger rises up into my throat, stopped just
in time before my huge disgust with him spills out
      onto the sidewalk
all around us, making a mess that later would end up on her.
I am watching her cry.
I am watching her tell us, her friends—
I am watching her face contort, in such sorrow, as she tells
on him,
again:

his latest affront leaking out
of her this way/that way theater mask mouth, in very few words,
for she does not have
many words
for this.
I am watching her shoulders, usually so straight and strong,
curve in around her heart,
like a small bird's wings will curve around its whole chest and belly
after falling.
I am watching as she tries to survive him,
again.
I am watching her with this man, this tall man,
            broad of shoulder, hairy face,
this man who cannot see her in any way
beyond his own desires, moment to moment;
this man who feels free to slam and break her life around her,
and sometimes even the life closest to her soul —
her body.
I am watching her be kind
to me
again,
and yet again,
as she is to so many, many of us, all the time
For this is who she is:
woman of Christ, singer, artist, harpist, mother,
sister, teacher, friend and serious play-outside-girl.
I am watching her, this unexpected bonus sibling God has given
to more than one of us orphan girls,
so fortunate are we.
I am watching her pain,
and this refrain that
has looped and looped on the broken record player of their home
for all the years I've known her—
though often she has tried to skip the needle
            off its black circling line,
so long to no avail...

but now...

but now...

and now…….

SKIP…!

SKREETCH…!

…I am watching her…
I am watching her courage,
her astonishing courage—
I am watching her speak her words so long unspoken
I am watching her tell our tribe in every honest way, THIS,
THIS is what has happened to me, behind our public music
and inside our secret songs.
I am watching her run for help, following
       her own well-laid breadcrumbs.
I am watching her let us fill the path behind her,
       so she can keep moving.
I am watching those who love her hold our hands up to this man
who has turned himself into a mad wild bear
by an alchemy of rage and selfishness,
and I am watching as we say to him *No!*
NO.
I am watching as we say to him,
We see you
and we see her and
you will not touch her again
despite your need to throw your fists into the parts of
yourself
that you hate,
that you have somehow fun-house-mirrored onto her.
No.
And I am watching her say, *NO:*
no more will I pay the price
for marriage with my skin and my bones, with my breath and my absence
from my own life; no longer may you exile me
from my own self.
I am watching her with love, with pride and with the
trembling frightened sister-hope I have felt
for her for so long, for all the goodness she deserves.

I am watching her in my prayers, with God;
I am watching her in my best visions for her green alive future.
I am watching her bring herself out of sleep
and into safety,
I am watching her save her life.

Twilight

"Oh what a wonderful soul so bright inside you.
Got power to heal the sun's broken heart,
power to restore the moon's vision too."

—*Aberjhani*

where the scar is

Vilma Ginzberg

touch me where I'm tender
touch me where I yield
touch me where you mustn't
    there the scar is

touch me where I'm hungry
touch me where I hurt
touch me where you mustn't
    where the scar is

touch me where I'm lonely
touch me where I weep
touch me where you mustn't
    where the scar is

touch me where I'm frozen
touch me where I cringe
touch me where you mustn't
    where the scar is

touch me in the never
touch me in the not
touch me in the nowhere
touch me touch me not

touch me when I'm ready
touch me when I ask
touch me when I trust you
    where the scar is

touch me with your kindness
touch me where I know
touch me make me tougher
    where the scar was

In the Darkest Times

Megan Ingrassia

In the darkest times, when it seems
there are no ears to hear the secrets I hide,
I hide my hope inside.
When it seems there is no escape from the one who takes,
I seal a seed of strength.
Though you would try to take it from me, I AM still beauty.
For a moment I forgot my meaning, I let you erase me.
Never again will I let your cruelty shape me.
I am woman.
I recreate me.

I heal myself with art. I heal myself first with my imagination. I use creativity to envision myself in new ways when I get stuck. When I feel weak and alone, I draw myself as a strong, independent figure. When I feel uptight and rigid, I draw myself as a flower, opening petal by petal. I use the art process to imagine myself with the qualities I lack and need to access. In this way I recreate myself as a piece of art, stroke by stroke. I see life as a creative process where I can reach toward the vision of my most authentic self, a fully realized masterpiece.

As an artist, I believe the most powerful way to heal myself is through artwork and recasting the images that captured my dreams so long ago, before the abuse. I observed that the images in my art making are often symbols which seem to erupt spontaneously from my unconscious, with a life of their own, demanding to be expressed. They can be a guiding beacon, or an honest statement of my psychic condition, or a warning. They serve as a reality check, showing me clearly what my illusions would readily hide.

They are silent friends, patient witnesses to the courage growing within. I used them at first unconsciously, then consciously as I began to recognize their meaning: to evoke the qualities I was lacking and surely needed. I came to believe the images were symbols that served the purpose of bringing me into alignment with my higher self, exposing my disowned part so that the whole could be seen and thus remembered. I now experience creating images as healing and transformative. I draw and paint self-portraits to facilitate conscious transformation.

Years ago, I was fighting depression, addiction, and neurosis. I blamed myself for all the fear that filled my family because that is what the tyrant in my home told me to believe. He had succeeded in turning me on myself, so that I would not see who was truly guilty. In a pool of self-loathing, I was unable for three years to break free from this man who terrorized my children and myself. But inside, images of hope were gestating.

For too long, I defended my abuser, soaking up the lies and deceit he fed me. Although I got sicker and more afraid every day, I kept putting my hope in him rather than in those whom I could trust. Although I'd been hospitalized because of him, my credit destroyed, and my friends pushed away, I clung to the man who told me he was there to protect me. In an art therapy class, an image emerged on paper to show me the truth.

Though I reached out to him for love, and though he looked right at me and told me that love is what he gave, the truth was now looking me in the eye with this image I colored. He was sucking the life out of me. He was draining the essence of who I was. I was so fragile, so raw and skinless, so defenseless. No matter how I felt about him, the truth was clear in this image. I grew weaker and he grew stronger.

The truth is: Love does not belittle, insult, or control. Love does not push when you are crying or bleeding. Love does not use or abuse. Love does not lie, cheat, and steal.

Though distant, I began to sense my true self from deep within. A year later I created a drawing that drew out the strength I was lacking. The image came in a dream. I had the limbs of a large jungle cat and I wore the Egyptian headdresses of both king and queen. Behind me hid an ocelot cub. Fierce, unafraid, and calm, this transformed image of myself stayed with me long after waking. As a single parent of two boys, the image showed me the dignity, strength, and grace required for the job. It evoked the energy of the protective lioness that guards her cubs at any cost. The image stayed on my walls through the abusive relationship, those knowing eyes silently speaking my true identity, reminding me who I was when I thought I'd been erased.

It took a lot of time. And it took a lot of courage. It took therapy and dedication. It took many painful moments to change myself into this creature that first only lived in my imagination. It took telling the people in my life the truth. It took really listening to my sons, feeling their pain, and promising I would never let anyone hurt them again. It took filing police reports and CPS reports to prevent him from harming other women and children in the future. And it took removing the thousand stinging tendrils of that man from my life, from my children, and from myself one by one.

But the results are beautiful. The images that emerge now reveal the unfolding of a woman in the healing process. The blossoming, petal by petal, day by day, challenge by challenge, and joy by joy, of living free of fear. I am reaching towards wholeness. I am embracing the beauty of being a woman, and the process of putting my family back together.

There is always hope, hiding in the dark. If only a tiny, hidden seed now, it can be watered with loving kindness, patience, and fierce protection. Imagine all the strength, intelligence, and grace you need, to do what must be done. That is hope, blossoming.

I Am Not Dead–Alias Jane Doe

Diane Madrigal

You broke my spirit, you shattered my dreams, you pierced my heart, you crushed me.

You took my love, you danced on my bed, you laughed, you joked and ridiculed me…you lied, you hid, you plotted, you stood tall over me and you pushed me to the ground.

You beat me, bruised me and defiled me with your words.

But

look

at

me…

Look at me!

I am not dead!

I am not defeated, nor defiled, I am not cursed, not damaged goods, I am not your stepping stool nor your carpet to walk on, I am not worthless, nor less than, I am not delusional or crazy, I am not good for nothing nor forsaken or mistaken or born to late nor should not have been born at all, I am not too big nor too small minded, I am not your bitch nor your toy, I am not replaceable, nor dispensable, I am not your boring whore.

I am not your boss who did not pay you your worth, I am not your mother who forgot to love you, I am not your ex-wife who tolerated you or any woman who you scapegoat.

I am not without tears or without soul, and I do have a penny to my name.

I am not your slave, your naïve, your cook, or nurse.

I am not ugly nor fat, not stupid, I am not to be broken, beaten, whipped, abused, or stolen, I am not to be tortured, laughed at, tied or lied too, I am not the walking dead.

Look

at

me...

Look at me!

I am not dead...

I am not dead!

I breathe, I cry, I pray, I laugh, I feel, I sing, I dance and scream, I smile and love and walk my path, I am a woman, I am whole.

I am honored, I am loved, I am chosen, I am gifted, I am delivered, I am free, I am strong, I am firm, I am special, I am whimsical, musical, beautiful.

I am deserving. I am redeemed. I am restored.

I am all things God created me to be, and out of his mouth, *out of His mouth*, I am.

I am not dead and you can't hurt me anymore.

Fractured

Juanita J. Martin

Mind splintered
from words that
dug into my skin

The lies, the taunts, threats of violence
you forced me to take
from you the master

I was your dog on a leash
always at your side
begging for acceptance

You branded me daily
with names that cut deeply,
scarring my soul

Took a pocketful of hope
my bruised and lonely heart
broke those chains for good

Now I'm free to love and be loved
free to lick my wounds
free to heal for the first time

My World Tipped Over

Juliana Marie Van Guilder

My name is Juliana, but people call me Julie. I'm thirteen, but in-side I'm four, because that's when my heart stopped beating. I want to think that I remember some great things about my dad. But I don't really know if I remember them because I remember, or I remember them because someone told me, and I created them in my mind. Some of my memories of my father have faded, even when I try hard to hold on to them. I have to think really hard about the way his voice sounds.

I remember that my dad was the tallest man in the world. He was so tall that he could put the angel on top of the Christmas tree without a ladder. He was so strong he could throw me up into the air and catch me with one hand. He could eat a Costco apple pie in one bite. One time, he ate my ice cream bar in ten seconds when I went to the potty. When I came back all that was left was the stick. He loved baseball and the Giants! He had every baseball card ever made and he shared them with me. I think about how his shirt smelled. I even kept a small bottle of his Polo cologne, so I can think of him. These memories I hold on to with both hands and heart.

On that day, when I was four, my mom, my sister, and I came out of the swimming pool, so we could take his clothes and his TV to his new place. Mom said we could go back to our pool when we were done. It had taken us an hour to blow it up and fill it with cold water and a couple of pots of hot water.

My daddy did not live with us anymore. He first lived in a hospital. We went there to see him. And then he lived with his friend, Ms. Teresa, and we would go there to see him. And then in a jail because he wasn't doing what he was supposed to do—we didn't go there. Finally, back to Ms. Teresa's house. When we got to her house, Mom started to unload his things from the back of the van and put them on the porch.

I saw daddy walking toward us. We were so happy to see him and started calling for him. My mom looked up, and she came quickly to the van. My sister and me climbed over the back seat to get out and gave him lots of hugs and kisses. His face was fuzzy, and I could feel all the tickles on my hands when I touched his face. He had been gone to jail for twenty-one days.

My sister asked him when he was coming home and he said soon. Soon was a long time to me. He told us to behave and to listen to mommy. He said he loved us and closed the back of the van. He tried to hug my mom, but my mom did not let him. She tried to pull away, but he had her by the arm. He was yelling and shouting loud. I was not sure what was happening, and I felt scared. My sister and I watched through the window as my mother tried to get away.

Daddy threw his hands in the air and everything he was holding went flying. I thought he was going to hit my mom. My mother came running. My dad stood there, still cussing. He was so loud that I thought it was thunder. Mom jumped into the van and zoomed away as she yelled at us to buckle up. We started to protest and call out to daddy, but he did not listen, and mom did not stop.

I saw my dad standing there and then I saw him running. I'm not sure where he was running. I wanted to go with him. I did not want to leave him, but I knew I could not stay. Something was wrong, really wrong. My mother was driving fast, and she was crying. She kept saying, "Oh, my God." The van came to a stop behind a tree. My mother got real quiet and turned off the van and the radio. She listened, and I looked around to see where we were, but we did not live there.

We waited for a few minutes, and I hoped that she was waiting for my dad, but she was hiding us. I know that now. She started the car, and we drove off again. I did not see him. I kept looking, but I did not see him. As we drove away, I felt sad. I missed him. I missed him reading me a story or carrying me on his shoulders, giving me bear hugs or sneaking donuts every morning before my school. I missed him and I did not understand why he could not live with us anymore.

We stopped at the light, and then I heard my dad's truck! I knew it was dad, even before I turned around. I recognized the sound of his truck three blocks away. I remember sitting in my car seat, and I saw my dad drive right next to our van. I smiled, and I waved, but he did not look at me. I could hear loud music and my dad yelling. He was yelling at my mom. His face was red and looked very angry. I had never seen him angry before; his face looked twisted and big. I felt scared.

I saw him pour his medicine into his mouth. I saw him drink his pink lemonade, and he threw the bottles at our window. He yelled that he was going to kill himself. My sister began to cry. I could hear everyone screaming and crying all at once. And I could hear my dad's voice the loudest. He sounded like a lion in the jungle. I heard my mom pleading with him to stop. But he did not. I started to scream for my dad, but he still did not stop.

The light turned green, and it felt like forever as we moved away from the truck. My mother turned left. I watched my dad come into our lane to follow us. I had never been afraid of my dad before. That day he was not like the dad I knew. He was trying to hurt us, and I did not understand why.

He kept pulling up alongside us. My mother quickly turned left in front of another car to get away from my dad and into the parking lot. I could hear his engine roaring behind us, getting louder and louder. I could hear the squealing of his tires and the squeak of his gears shifting in his big truck. He was revving the engine. I felt a crunch—something hit our van.

I could hear other cars braking and honking and screeching. I could hear people in the parking lot screaming as he continued to hit the van over and over again. I wanted it to stop. I kept falling in my seat to the left and then to the right and then forward. My sister was screaming, and I cried for my mom to help me, but she kept driving fast, making many turns, trying to get away. My sister kept screaming to call the police, but my mom did not stop. She kept swerving and stopping each time he hit us and then she would start again, trying to go faster than him.

There were lots of cars and people walking. I could see them. They were staring at us with eyes wide open, some were pointing and others running. They could see us, but my mom did not stop. My car seat tipped over, and I was hanging there, screaming—seeing the world pass by from the side view of my tipped chair, listening to the windows breaking, everything flying past my face. I felt the glass hit my face and my legs, but my mom did not stop.

My mother looked back at me and in her face, I could see she wanted to help me, but she kept driving crazy. I tried to reach her and pulled at the seat in front of me. The van came to a stop, and my sister came to get me out of the car seat. I heard her yell at my sister to get help as she jumped out of the van calling my father's name.

We stared out the window for what seemed like forever, and I saw my mom walk toward my dad. I wanted to go too, but I felt my sister's hands pulling me toward the other door. She pulled me out and toward the people who were standing around in the parking lot watching us go in circles.

I heard the loud roar of my dad's truck, as my mother got closer to him. I looked over my shoulder as my sister dragged me away to safety. The people in the parking lot grabbed my sister and me and pulled us out of the way.

I watched as my dad chased my mother in his truck, and I saw her jump out of the way. I heard the crunch as he hit the van where my mother was standing. It looked like she flew in the air, but he missed her. I kept yelling at him to stop! "Stop, Daddy. Stop!" But he did not listen. He could not hear me.

I heard his engine get louder and louder. Daddy's big black blazer was coming toward us. The one I used to drive while sitting on my dad's lap, the one with my car seat in the front seat, where my dad would let me sit when my mom was not around. The one with Cher singing when we would all sing together,

I heard people yelling and screaming and the roar got louder and louder. I couldn't hear anything or see my mother anymore, just the shiny grill that I used to help my dad wash. He came closer and closer to where we were standing. I felt someone pull me off my feet and we fell down. I saw my dad's truck hit the car where we were standing.

I heard yelling and crying and screaming and I don't remember if it was me or everyone around me. I covered my ears, but I could still hear the sirens and more crashing. I looked for my mom. But I could not see her; then I saw her standing on the truck step. I saw my father grab her by the shirt and pull her into the truck. I heard people screaming, "Don't do it. Don't do it. Don't go! Run! RUN!!

But I watched. My heart was pounding so loud. My mom went inside the truck and was talking to my dad. I heard the sirens. The police cars came, and I saw my mom jump out of the truck. I remember wanting to run to her, to get away from the people who were holding me. I kicked and screamed to let me go. I screamed for my mom as loud as I could. I screamed

"MOOOOOM!" I can't explain what I felt, only that I was shaking and I couldn't breathe!

The police pulled out their guns. I'd seen on TV what that meant, and I kept waiting for the bullet. My heart was pounding in my ears, then it stopped. Everything around me froze in time and moved like in slow motion.

The next thing I saw was my mother running toward us. She grabbed us, my sister and me, right off the ground. She tried to run holding us, but someone grabbed us and pulled us all down. She was checking us, crying and screaming in a voice I have never heard—so high pitched, shaky—it was like she was wounded. Her shirt was all torn, her hair was flying, but she pulled us to her and under her, with her arms and body over us, close to the ground, until the ambulance came and took us away. I saw my brother look into the ambulance and then my uncle, when the ambulance took us.

I have that memory. I have those flashbacks, I feel the pain, and I get lost. I cry and I die a little inside when I think of the dad I had, and the dad who went away. I loved him, and I lost him. My mother cried for years. I would hear her. I would cry and hide my tears. I don't understand. I can't change what happened. I can't make it better or different than it was. It hurt and it still hurts. I lost all my family, my dad, my brother, my aunts and my uncles. I lost so many people over and over again. Everyone was divided and blamed my mom for what happened.

Sometimes I think no one understands—that I am all alone. I tell my story, because I am lost somewhere. Something is missing from what I remember. They gave my dad thirty-seven years in prison, where he died three years ago, then my grandfather died, and then my grandmother. Sometimes, I don't feel like getting up or talking to anyone. I smile. I laugh and I get mad, but it doesn't change what I remember most.

I don't know if it is right or wrong. But I loved my dad, and I love him still. I don't like what he did to us. I just know that there was something terribly wrong with him that nobody could change. I used to feel pain and suffering every time I remembered what he did. When I see other kids with their dads, or when their dads pick them up from school, or when I just needed to feel safe, I think about my dad: the dad he was, the dad he became, and the dad I will never have again.

What I learned is that one single day did not make up his whole life. What I learned is that I can forgive him, and it is okay to love him and miss him. What I know is that when my memory seems to fade, I tell my mom and she shares the best stories of my dad with me, because there was good in him.

My mother would take us to his gravesite, and it was hard. For a long time it was hard. But now I think I have come to some kind of peace about it, maybe because I have made sense of what I remember. Maybe it is because I wrote about it and cried about it. I am not sure, but now every time I visit his gravesite, I am peaceful. I can sit there and think of him. My mom will sit with us and tell us some of our favorite stories about Dad.

I finally feel like I can be happy again. I feel relieved that my dad is at peace and in a better place. It took me nine years to find that out. People can recover from domestic violence even when it feels like the whole world doesn't understand.

I want to help my family and other kids like me understand. I want them to get better.

An Unfathomable Truth

Deborah Taylor-French

No right to life.
Battered in the womb, a baby born in a maelstrom of violence.
Unresponsive at fourteen days old and under five pounds,
      she's losing weight.
Counselors risk a call. We sign the foster care form.
Infant thigh bones show clearly, she may die.
Dawn blue eyes lock on me as she guzzles three ounces,
she wakes every two hours, screaming for more.
We cradle her, singing, rocking, hoping.
That week, she gains a pound.
An adoption expert states, "No chance in the world."
After a year of desperate loving, "Free," says a judge.
She's sixteen. We're parents.
Marvels do happen.

Losing Abby

Robyn Anderson

A band of people gathered at the stop light, waiting to cross the street, to enter a building that would change their lives: the County Superior Courthouse. The band of people was to be their family.

My older sister, Abby, was three years old and I was three months old when we moved into foster care. We'd waited almost four years for a forever family. During those years, various case managers bounced us between six different foster homes. I remember them as nice homes with nice people. But we always knew they were temporary to us…that we were temporary to them. Most kids in foster care feel temporary. And finally we weren't temporary. We had a home.

🌿

Abby and I had many happy years together with our new family, gardening, laughing, and dancing. My most comforting time was when we would sit in front of the fireplace, watching cooking shows or movies, playing board games, guessing whose back could take the heat of the flames the longest. So many times, though, I could sense that feeling comfortable made Abby feel horribly uncomfortable.

I was only nine years old when everything began unraveling. I could see that, more and more often, loud noises would send Abby places none of us understood. She would startle at every sound, every movement, every door and window…opening and closing.

Abby told me she would think of ways to break away from fun times with our family. She said she needed to break away because she was feeling too happy, and she had to stop the too-happy feelings and return to the more comfortable, hurt feelings of her early years. So she would secretly hurt herself to stop the happy and to feel a distant, but familiar pain.

She would pull at her eyebrows until there were only patches of hair. She would scratch her left forearm with her right hand fingernails until it bled, and she would keep scratching so it kept

~ 117 ~

bleeding. She kept findings ways to hurt herself, to continue breaking away from us. It was hurting and breaking all of us.

Still, despite this peculiar and puzzling behavior, I thought we'd be okay. And it was, until it really wasn't. In a single night, everything changed as Abby's demons came calling and she went crazy. She was seeing things and hearing words only she could see and hear.

The ambulance came and took Abby.

The band of people gathered in the waiting room of the adolescent psychiatric hospital. Some in the band found hospitals uncomfortable, with rooms full of the disturbed. Like many families of children from foster care, everyone hoped they could help the children thread their way from a traumatized early beginning into full and meaningful adulthood. But nothing was holding together.

After the first couple of hospitalizations, the cozy fires my dad made for us were less frequent and the comfort meals my mom made for us were less comforting. Overall there was less warmth, less food, and more alarm. Abby spent the next five years in numerous psychiatric hospitals and residential treatment facilities. We visited often and my parents had weekly therapy sessions with her (in person when she was close by and over the phone when she was far away). I spoke with her occasionally during "social calls." It was difficult to know what to say as the sister I knew was no longer.

Abby tried to come back to our family many times during her treatment years. The visits were always cut short when the voices came calling, taunting her to hurt herself because she didn't deserve a family and never did, and that she should hurt anyone who tried to help her. She would return to the facility, usually by ambulance, and we would start over, again. And we would keep trying, trying to help her heal from her early wounds.

At times it seemed the medicine and therapy were working, and once again we would be all right. But the voices kept returning to Abby and everything, once again, fell apart.

The original band of people scattered in different places and in different directions and for different reasons. The countless years were painful and over-

whelming. It affected families and altered the course of friendships.

As I reflect back, I will always believe we lost Abby because of the abuse and neglect our birth parents inflicted on her. I guess I was the luckier one—in an odd way—to have been placed in foster care so soon after my birth. Most people would find that hard to believe. But being older, Abby was with them longer, shouldering their violence and harboring unseen voices that came and went...and probably still come and go.

It's been twelve years, eight months, and sixteen days since Abby left through her bedroom window, during—what turned out to be—her last home visit. She never came back.

And while I wait for her to come home, I'm able to find comfort in the memories of the many fires my dad made for us and the many times we gathered near the fireplace as a family. I'm able to find peace and warmth in the dancing flames of a fire my family helped me build for myself. Mostly I feel comfortable with and comforted by that inner fire, yet sometimes the flames fuel my sense of rejection from foster families, of betrayal by my birth parents, of abandonment by my sister. But while the flames may cause me painful pause, I continue to learn to tame them.

🔥

The band of people remains in my life, those who loved and those who could not, at least in memory. But there is a difference now: I am the one in the courthouse who can protect and support children who have been hurt, neglected, or abused—as an attorney and child advocate.

Domestic Violence in Three Poems
Ann Carranza

I. Scars

His right fist slams into my eye
and I see stars though my tears.
Bruises mark my face, arms, chest, belly.
I'm terrified—I cannot move, I cannot run.
I'm trapped behind the wheel of a
car, my long hair fisted in his left hand
when his right grabs me by the throat.

With his back to the windshield,
he raves. Spittle spraying from his lips
hits my face.

Memories of those years, years, years ago
still fill my eyes with tears.

I don't remember, remember, remember
why his crazed mind believed I
should be punished.

I learned last year
he died—the victim of a hit and run.
I felt relief.

He's no longer a threat to any woman—
those fists stilled at last.
That poor, sad life
and rotten childhood
provide no excuses.

He's gone
but these three decades later
I still feel
the fists pound
and wonder
what I did
to deserve such pain.

II. Learning curve

I got out…damn, it took years
but I was lucky.
His stays didn't last long
then he'd be gone for six
months, sometimes more.

He almost died, the time he broke the
window to get into
my house.
I walked in after work
to the meat-locker scent
of fresh blood.

He was barely breathing.
I called 9-1-1
and took the towel
off his arm.

My sight dimmed
when I saw the wound.

He stopped breathing,
then restarted.
The emergency operator
stayed on the line,
talking to me
until police, fire, ambulance
arrived.

The doctor saved his arm,
they replaced his blood.
But no one could heal
his violent soul or
cure his hatred for women.

III. Forward to Joy

Yes, it did take years
and yes, I do bear scars
but
he didn't take my life.

I celebrate
the small things—
bullfrogs and butterflies.

I celebrate
the loving ones—
my husband, my sons, my grandsons, my friends.

I celebrate
learning and knowledge,
college and career.

The scars are but a
reminder
that I am, luckily and completely, alive.

Hope

Sher Christian

The actions of those who are unconscionable
so defile the world with cruelty, greed, insanity,
lack of humanity toward living beings,
I fear even the wild night winds cannot cleanse
this dark force from the earth.
Yet the sweet scent of morning dawns fresh
each day. I put hurt and anger
in the fire of forgiveness,
open the blossom of my heart
to love.
I offer prayers and songs of praise
for the beauty of the twisting oaks,
the harsh cries of the fox and geese,
the power of my courage.

Driving Free

Michelle Wing

Melissa Etheridge is playing on the radio, and the car is filled with conversation and laughter. We are cruising south down the coast on Highway One on a brilliant California late afternoon, as waves crash into the rocks below us.

I am at the steering wheel of my black Nissan. My passengers are three gay men, among them my best buddy Nick and his new beau, the one he has just hooked up with at the weekend retreat we have been attending near Gualala. The combined energy of new love, an infusion of nature after our usual urban life in San Francisco, and the giddiness we often feel from talking late into the night has us pink-cheeked and euphoric.

At one point, as the car hugs the tight curves of the road, swaying us back and forth in rhythm, everyone falls into a comfortable silence. And then Nick says, "I feel really safe with you, Michelle. You're a good driver."

My breath stops in my chest, and for one instant my eyesight blurs. I am catapulted back to the memory of my timid, former self, who was afraid to sit in the driver's seat.

I met a girl. At times, she was light and playful, and we enjoyed each other's company. Other times, she was deeply troubled. I was drawn to that injured part of her, too. I thought that maybe, just maybe, I could reach in and help. I did not know I would be destroyed in the process. I did not know she would systematically trample every piece of goodness in me she could find.

The destruction started out simply. She lied. She lied to her boss about missing work, saying an aunt had passed away. At parties, she lied about what she had studied in school. When asked who her favorite author was, she would reply, "Virginia Woolf," even though she had never read anything written by her. When I tried to reason with her, tell her there was no point in hiding behind these falsehoods, she refused to listen.

She began to have strong opinions about everything to do with me. She commented on what I wore. She did not like my Converse tennis shoes. She liked it when I wore dresses when we went out dancing. She preferred my hair a certain way. When we were with others, she expected certain behavior. She wanted me to appear smart, but not talk too much. She liked to show me off, but would then put me down in front of others. If I made a misstep, she would not hesitate to speak sharply to me in public.

And then, of course, there was the car. She used the automobile as a place to express her anger and hostility towards the world. One night I got a call to pick her up in an emergency room. She keyed a man's truck in a parking lot because he beat her to a parking space. The guy saw her and came out with fists flying, not realizing, at first glance, that she was a woman. She was righteously indignant about the incident, wanting to press charges against him for assault. He was equally furious, wanting her to pay for the damage to his truck.

When we drove, she frequently tailgated, swerved, careened around, and frightened me. But if I showed any fear or other emotion, she yelled at me. If I was at the steering wheel, she spent the entire trip criticizing my skills, telling me I was too hesitant, too slow, not paying attention, too timid. Yet she absolutely insisted I drive half of the time. We frequently went on weekend road trips, which meant gut-wrenching anxiety for me, as I either drove under her hypercritical eye, or was a scared passenger, never knowing whether or not she would be flipping off a cop or aggravating some other poor motorist.

Why would I stick around for this treatment? At first, it was because I thought I was strong enough. I knew her history. She had been horrifically abused as a child. I wanted to heal that wound. I wanted to be the one who could love her enough. As her own emotionally abusive behavior began with me, as it slowly crept into our relationship, it caught me off guard. I had been a victim before, but my abuser had been a man. I wasn't expecting it from a woman. Even though the violence this time had not yet reached a physical level, by the time I realized what was happening, the dismantling of my core self had progressed too far. I no longer had a safe place to retreat to, a reservoir of courage to draw upon. By then, it was too late.

I did finally find the strength to leave. But only after she had stalked me, tried to get me fired from my job, forced me out of my home, hired an attorney, attempted to serve a restraining order on me, and took me through the court system.

For months afterward, in hiding, I startled at sudden

sounds. I looked over my shoulder, screened my calls, spoke tremulously, picked at my food, slept badly, and trusted no one. And when I drove my car to my new job, I gripped the steering wheel tightly, my back erect, eyes locked on the road. Driving had become a heart-pounding trauma. All the pleasure had been sucked out of it.

Now, in this magical moment on Highway One, with Nick's words, I realize a shift has happened. There is healing. I allow myself to hear him again. "I feel really safe with you, Michelle. You're a good driver."

I remember. I like driving. This is what it feels like. The road, opening up in front of me, taking me wherever I want to go. An adventure, new places, opportunities. I am a good driver.

I am driving free.

After the Violence: Haiku Affirmations

Kitty Wells

Breathing long and slow
I return to my center.
Its pure love heals me.

It was not my fault.
I accept myself fully.
It was not my fault.

Heavy shame coat
grows wings and flies away.
Body and soul lighten.

A child inside
whispers, "I'm afraid."
I hug her closely.

Carrying tools now
to face the truth. I breathe in
blessed compassion.

I know it happened.
My mind is not playing tricks.
I was victimized.

Learning to discern,
I trust my own perceptions.
I am in control.

Sharing my story,
I speak my truth and survive.
Life has more color

My Body Remembered
Ann Hutchinson

Writing a memoir for *Changing Hurt to Hope* three years ago, in 2010, was the beginning of what became the most amazing personal odyssey of renewal and growth I've ever experienced. I wrote "Strangled" about being attacked by my first husband when I was five months pregnant. Two weeks after writing and reading that painful memory in public, I traveled to my abuser's convalescent home in Washington State with my daughter and her kids. She wanted to visit her father, who was dying from cirrhosis and liver cancer, and needed help with the kids. She had not seen her father since I left him when she was two.

I spent my birthday watching the kids in the rental car while she spent time with him in the convalescent home. She came out to get the kids one last time to say goodbye before we left. I went with her. I don't know why. To face my fear? He asked me for a hug. "I think I remember things differently than you do," I said as I sat as close to the exit as possible, excusing myself as soon as my granddaughter got fussy.

He died a week later. After seeing the results of his addiction, it reaffirmed that separating my children from their father was the right thing. But I found myself questioning why I would not let myself leave what had become another unhealthy relationship, this time with emotional abuse, which is often more insidious. My second husband had his own demons that he was unable to conquer, and he was, after ten years of trying, simply giving up, and dragging me down into his despair. I left him six months after that Washington trip.

At the end of that year, I fit pieces to a puzzle together that further changed my life. In 1988, the next time I was pregnant after the strangling, was the beginning of my back problems, a condition that persisted for twenty years. I finally had surgery in May 2010, but muscles in my back continued to seize up for no apparent reason.

My body remembered.

If it could speak, it would have said, five years after the strangling, "Oh, we're pregnant again. We had better brace ourselves for the strangling," as it clenched the muscles in my back. Trauma like that, even though we file it in the far reaches of our consciousness, never remembering it unless unlocked through treatment, doesn't stay forgotten. Our bodies remember.

That trauma can come back like an old football injury or a war wound. And can plague us at every turn. Our bodies don't know the difference between one trauma and the next. Trauma is trauma. And it hurts. Over and over again.

The good news is that when I put all of this together I happened to be friends with someone who practices Somatic Experiencing. She took me, mentally and emotionally, back to that Washington visit just before he died. "What would you do if you could react differently now?" she asked. You see, when the fight or flight mechanism is stymied...when we can't do either...we freeze. And freeze the trauma in our bodies.

At first I said, "Run!" And then I thought harder. I remembered wanting to run. But there was another response I shut down as unthinkable and impossible at the time. More base. Unbidden and unanswered. I wanted to punch him in the face. Then run.

In somatic experiencing, you act out that thing you couldn't before—in slow motion. That lets your body know that that loop is closed. The danger has been answered. The threat is over.

I have since taken back my life. Embraced the little girl who got sidelined by childhood trauma I hadn't even remembered (surfaced through SE). I understand now that I was fed a diet of blame and shame that predisposed me to settle for abusive relationships. Today, I am a dancing queen. A vital woman, full of energy, and potential, and a strong voice. And I'm married to the love of my life. We just waltzed back down the aisle at our wedding in mid-August, expressing our passion for dance. We met doing the thing we both love.

He never abuses me in any way. He respects me and my opinions, and gives me room to grow. And it all started here. Because I dared to remember, to write about my trauma, and find healing.

This Heart

Janet Vallance

She is a superstar.
That duct tape is tucked
tight around her leaking seams.
She will not fail me.
She creaks and moans
and pulls my hair.
I tell her she is so bold.
I tell her she has nine lives.
I tell her she must prepare for the unveiling
of the new love
of the new life.
She must be young for the open house.
She must be young for the trips I have planned
for the tropics.

When this is all over
I am going to buy her the prettiest dress.
I am going to bring her a puppy
and hide polished rubies in her pockets.

I am going to take her to the river
everyday, everyday, everyday
and let the cold sound
of water over rocks mend her skin.

Acknowledgements

No book comes into the world alone; this is especially true of anthologies, a collaborative effort by definition. *Cry of the Nightbird: Writers Against Domestic Violence* is no exception, and any list of people we thank will be inadequate.

That said, we offer our gratitude to all the writers who allowed us to consider their stories and poems—both those whose work is included in the final publication and those whose work is not. For all the writers in the Changing Hurt to Hope project, it took courage to relive their own traumas and to write about it in a way that communicated their experiences to readers. Special thanks go to the contributing authors for participating in the editorial process.

In defining the book and giving it a professional assessment, we are grateful to early readers of our book proposal, Laurie McLean and Gordon Warnock of Foreword Literary. Madeleine Keegan O'Connell, Chief Executive Officer, YWCA Sonoma County, has been a key supporter of the years-long project that created this book and has our sincere gratitude for endorsing it. YWCA's volunteer coordinators, Donata Mikulik (2010-2012) and Misty Bastoni (2012-present), and fund development manager Mary Beth Cerjan Falk, have also been critical members of the Changing Hurt to Hope team.

We thank Shirlee Zane for her strong and supportive introduction. We thank Carrie Nassif, whose evocative photographs enhance the book sections and Sonja Bauer whose art defines the cover. And finally, we thank Carol Hightshoe of WolfSinger Publications for publishing the book and contributing much of her technical expertise in layout and book design.

About Domestic Violence:
A Basic Introduction

What Is Domestic Violence?

It is important to define exactly what we are talking about when discussing domestic violence.* The term has both specific legal meanings, and also common usages in the advocacy and support fields. Legally, in the California Penal Code, domestic violence is abuse committed against an adult or minor who is a spouse, former spouse, cohabitant, former cohabitant, or a person with whom the person has had a child, or is having or has had a dating relationship. The focus here, then, is on the relationship between the two parties.

Social service agencies like the YWCA Sonoma County define domestic violence as threatening behavior by an intimate partner attempting to seek control over another.

When most people hear the term "domestic violence," they think of physical abuse. But the spectrum of violence is much broader than that in reality, as any survivor knows. Violence takes many shapes and forms.

Abuse can be:

• Verbal (name calling, put-downs, angry tirades, silent treatment)

• Emotional and psychological (jealousy, controlling behavior, stalking, spying, isolation of the victim from family and friends, psychological manipulation, threats of impending physical violence by breaking things in close proximity to the victim, threats with a knife or gun, threats to harm children, friends, family, and/or pets, or threats of suicide)

• Financial (control of all the money, expectation that the victim earn all the money, destruction of the victim's credit)

• Religious (forcing the victim to practice a religion, not allowing the victim to follow her religious beliefs)

• Sexual (refusal to use birth control, promiscuity, unprotected sex, forcing the victim to participate in degrading sexual acts, rape)

 • Physical (depriving the victim of sleep or food, pushing, slapping, hitting, punching, biting, kicking, hair pulling, burning, stabbing, and worse, up to and including homicide)

The Cycle of Violence

Anyone who has ever been in an abusive relationship will recognize the "Cycle of Violence," the consistent pattern that domestic violence falls into, repeating over and over again.

It starts with the "tension-building" phase. During this time, communication in the relationship is beginning to break down, and the abuser is slowly escalating angry or manipulative behavior. Victims often describe their feelings during this time as akin to "walking on eggshells," being oh-so-careful, trying hard to do just the right thing so that nothing will trigger the impending disaster.

But it is no use. There is always an explosion, the moment of abuse. In the beginning, it might only be a tirade. Later, as the cycle repeats, the abuse gradually worsens, moving steadily towards physical violence.

After the abuse happens, there is a period of calm, sometimes referred to as "the honeymoon phase," although this bears no resemblance to a real honeymoon, as this one is filled with false promises. The abuser may act like nothing happened, or conversely, will go out of his way to apologize, even showering his partner with gifts to make up for his previous actions. The first time, this can be enchanting, and the partner will want to believe that the ugly behavior was an anomaly and will never happen again.

The truth, though, is that the cycle, in all likelihood, will repeat. Sometimes a cycle can last a few hours, sometimes a year. Each time, the explosion phase will be more dramatic, the calm period shorter. The cycle keeps going, trapping the victim in its center, until it is like a whirling eddy that never ends.

Why Does She Stay?

Hopefully after reading the poems, stories, and personal narratives in this book, this common question will be easier for you to answer, because you will have seen the incredible complexity of the situations women and men find themselves in.

It generally takes abused partners six to seven attempts before they leave for good. There are many reasons for this. She may still truly love her partner, and believe that the relationship can be saved. She wants to do it for the children, so they can live with both parents. It may be a financial consideration; she's unsure how she can support herself out on her own. She may have nowhere to go; often women who leave end up homeless, struggling to feed themselves and their children. There may be pressure from other family members to return, to try to work things out. The members of her faith community may be encouraging her to remain true to her marriage vows. Perhaps she is unsure of herself, and her ability to be independent, because of years spent listening to the belittling words of her batterer. Or maybe she left, and her batterer found her and stalked her, so there was no peace, and she simply became tired, gave up, and returned home.

The most important thing to remember is that only the person who is leaving a relationship knows when it is the right time. Women do leave, and go on to build bright, new futures. But escaping is also the riskiest moment, the time when a woman's life is in the greatest jeopardy, when most homicides happen. Only she knows when it is safe.

Who Is Affected?

In Sonoma County last year, law enforcement responded to more than three thousand domestic violence calls. It is the leading cause of injury to local women. Nationwide, one in four women will experience domestic violence at some point in her lifetime. Eighty-five percent of victims are women, with an estimated 1.3 million women assaulted by their intimate partners each year.

We do know that this violence crosses all lines: It affects people regardless of gender, age, economic status, race, religion, nationality, educational background, or sexual orientation.

One in fourteen men will suffer from domestic violence. Overwhelmingly, for men, this violence is committed in same-sex relationships. However, we also know that male victims underreport because of the stigma of being a male survivor, the fear of not being believed, and a lack of societal and family support.

Intimate partner violence happens in our schools, too. One

in three teens know a friend who has been hit, kicked, slapped, choked, or physically hurt by their partner. More than 22 percent of female victims and 15 percent of male victims experience violence for the first time between the ages of eleven and seventeen. And nearly half the female victims (45 percent) and more than one-third of male victims (39 percent) were between the ages of eighteen and twenty-four when they first suffered abuse.

It is not just the teen, young adult, and adult victims who are affected. Thirty to sixty percent of the perpetrators of domestic violence also abuse the children in their homes. Boys who witness domestic violence are twice as likely to abuse their own partners and children when they become adults.

Our society as a whole is also impacted. The cost of intimate partner violence exceeds $5.8 billion each year, $4.1 billion of which is for direct medical and mental health services. Victims of domestic violence lost almost eight million days of paid work because of the violence they suffered at the hands of their partners in 2013. This is a problem that reaches into every corner of our communities, and is something that we cannot afford to ignore.

*In this essay, for the sake of convenience, victims and survivors are referred to as "she," and abusers and batterers as "he," with the understanding that although women are statistically more likely to be the victims, both genders may be in either role, and sometimes in both roles, in the case of same-sex relationships.

What You Can Do:
Resources for Domestic Violence

The YWCA Sonoma County was founded in 1975 by a group of local women who volunteered their own homes as an underground network of safe houses. The YWCA Safe House, a confidential emergency residence, providing food, clothing, and shelter, plus treatment and intervention, was created the next year. It was among the first fifteen such shelters in the United States.

Two years later, the YWCA established its Child Care Services Program to provide services to children at risk due to exposure to domestic violence and child abuse. A Special Place continues to provide the only therapeutic preschool in Sonoma County, serving children affected by the traumas of early exposure to domestic violence in the home.

Today, the YWCA Sonoma County's Domestic Violence Services Program provides onsite services in Santa Rosa through its Safe House, A Special Place Preschool, and at the Family Justice Center. Services include:

Crisis Hotline: Available twenty-four hours, the crisis line serves survivors by offering immediate intervention, advocacy, counseling, and legal advice, as well as referrals to resources in the community. Call (707) 546-1234.

The Safe House: The confidential safe house provides eight weeks of shelter for women and their children fleeing violence with legal services, support groups, children's advocacy, and intensive case management.

Adobe Aftercare Program: This two-year supportive care program for clients moving on from the Safe House allows them to further their healing and helps them create a life free from violence by continuing with case management (referrals, safety planning, goal setting), counseling, court accompaniment, and workshops on topics such as financial education, parenting, self-care, and self defense.

A Special Place: The only therapeutic preschool in Sonoma County, A Special Place serves up to thirty three- to five-year-olds daily; each child is provided with breakfast, lunch, and a healthy snack through the Free and Reduced Lunch program.

Counseling and support: Counseling is available for women and children in the Safe House and in the Adobe Aftercare Program. There are also community support groups, with topics such as defining domestic violence, red flags, safety planning, effects of domestic violence on children, why women stay, power and control, and the cycle of violence. Call the hotline to register.

Outreach: Staff and volunteers from the YWCA go out into the community to talk about domestic violence, its impacts, and warning signs. They speak at service groups, community events, and anywhere there is an opportunity and a need. There is also a Teen Dating Violence program, bringing talks into local schools.

Family Justice Center: The Family Justice Center is a model for providing victims with a single point of access to navigate the legal system. Serving victims of domestic violence, elder abuse, stalking, and sexual assault, it is located at 2755 Mendocino Ave., Suite 100, Santa Rosa, (707) 565-8255. Onsite partners include the YWCA, Verity (for sexual assault), Council on Aging, Inter Tribal Council, Legal Aid, Catholic Charities, the Sonoma County DA's Office victim services, and law enforcement, with detectives from the Sonoma County Sheriff's Office and the Santa Rosa Police Department.

Volunteering: The YWCA offers two forty-hour training sessions twice yearly to those interested in becoming volunteers for the agency. Each year more than 100 volunteers provide 10,000 hours of service to the YWCA, giving presentations, working at the Family Justice Center, helping with court accompaniment, assisting at the Safe House and A Special Place, and more. For information, contact Misty Bastoni, volunteer coordinator, at (707) 303-8401 or mbastoni@ywcasc.org.

Other *California* Domestic Violence (DV) Resources:

California Partnership to End Domestic Violence: (www. cpedv.org/Resources) has DV hotlines and services for the state of California.

Women's Law website: (www.womenslaw.org) provides DV services, including law enforcement, for the state of California, listed by city. Go to *Where to Find Help, Help in Your State*, and select *California*.

Safe at Home Program: (www.sos.ca.gov/safeathome) is a confidential, free post office box provided by the California Secretary of State, to allow DV survivors the freedom to receive first-class mail, open a bank account, complete confidential name changes, register to vote, enroll their children in school, and more, without fear of being tracked down by their batterer.

California State Victim Compensation: (www.vcgcb.ca.gov) reimburses victims for costs related to crimes, such as medical and dental treatment, mental health services, income loss, job retraining, home security, relocation, and crime scene cleanup. Victim advocates will also help victims find emergency food, clothing and shelter, file for a temporary restraining order, attend court hearings, and refer them to other resources.

National DV Resources:

24-hour National Domestic Violence Hotline: (800) 799-SAFE (7233), connects callers to local DV programs for those who are having trouble finding them locally.

National Teen Dating Violence Hotline: (866) 331-9474 (or text "loveis" to 22522).

GLBTQ Domestic Violence Project: (800) 832-1901 is a 24-hour hotline for GLBTQ intimate partner violence.

The GLBTQ Domestic Violence Project: (www.glbtqdvp.org) provides information, statistics, and brochures on the particular issues of DV that face the gay / lesbian / bisexual / transgender / queer community.

Women's Law website: (www.womenslaw.org) provides tips on staying safe, preparing for court, learning about abuse, helping others, and finding resources at the local, state, and federal level. It also provides a comprehensive listing of laws, broken down by state, with sections on restraining orders, custody, parental kidnapping, divorce, housing laws, workplace protection, gun laws, crimes, and suing your abuser, which includes federal and tribal laws.

Alianza, National Latino Alliance for the Elimination of Domestic Violence: (www.dvalianza.org) has information, statistics, and brochures in English and Spanish, about the particular aspects of DV that impact the Latino community.

Institute on Domestic Violence in the African American Community: (www.idvaac.org) provides information and statistics about the particular issues facing African American communities dealing with DV.

Mending the Sacred Hoop/Working to End Violence Against Native American Women: (mshoop.org) has information and downloadable training guides for use in Native American communities dealing with DV issues.

Recommended Reading

Domestic Violence

The Domestic Violence Sourcebook, Dawn Berry, 3rd edition, 2000. A comprehensive, compassionate look at domestic violence—including historical, psychological, social, familial, and legal issues—this well-organized, accessible book offers information on prevention and recovery, along with practical steps for escaping a violent domestic situation.

The Verbally Abusive Relationship: How to Recognize It and How to Respond, Patricia Evans, 3rd edition, 2010. How to recognize abuse when it happens and respond safely and appropriately.

Specific Communities

Mejor sola que mal acompañada: para la mujer golpeada / For the Latina in an Abusive Relationship (edición bilingüe) (Spanish), Myrna Zambrano, 1st edition, 1993. Writing in both Spanish and English, Zambrano, a Mexican-American bilingual counselor for battered Latinas, offers victims of family violence encouragement, sensitive understanding and valuable advice: how to get into a shelter for battered women, how to find police protection, how to prevent a husband from kidnapping the children. She also addresses the Latin woman's particular problems—unsympathetic police officers, lack of immigration documentation, the need for interpreters, and includes a chapter for social service workers who help Latinas, a glossary of legal terms, and a bibliography.

Violencia domestica–Deteccion, prevencion, y ayuda / Domestic Violence–Detection, Prevention and Help (Spanish Edition), Celso William Chignoli, 2011. This resource will help create awareness of domestic violence in the Hispanic culture. Available only in Spanish.

Abused Men: The Hidden Side of Domestic Violence, Philip W. Cook, 2nd edition, 2009. Investigates the evidence for abuse of men as a significant social problem, and tells victims how to get help, with sections on laws, support groups, crisis intervention programs and more.

Intimate Betrayal: Domestic Violence in Lesbian Relationships, Ellyn Kaschak, 2002. Why is woman-on-woman violence so often ignored or discounted? This book uncovers the hidden problem of lesbians who hurt their intimate partners. This long-needed book brings together theory, practice, and research to suggest new and fruitful ways to understand, prevent, and treat this common problem.

Effects of Domestic Violence on Children and Families

When Dad Hurts Mom: Helping Your Children Heal the Wounds of Witnessing Abuse, Lundy Bancroft, 2005. Bancroft draws on sixteen years of counseling men who abuse women and as a custody evaluator and child-abuse investigator to offer sound advice to women who are abused by their partners and are concerned about the impact on their children.

Family and Friends' Guide to Domestic Violence: How to Listen, Talk and Take Action When Someone You Care About is Being Abused, Elaine Weiss, 2003. "...offers practical answers to extraordinarily complex questions raised by abuse. She speaks to all of us—including men."—Esta Soler, founder and president, Family Violence Prevention Fund.

Aftermath and Recovery from Domestic Violence

Trauma and Recovery: The Aftermath of Violence—from Domestic Abuse to Political Terror, Judith Hermann, reprint 1997. A groundbreaking book originally written in 1992 that changed the way we think about traumatic events and trauma victims. Hermann draws on her own cutting-edge research in domestic violence, as well as on the vast literature of combat veterans and victims of political terror, to show the parallels between private terrors such as rape and public traumas such as terrorism. The book puts individual experience in a broader political frame, arguing that psychological trauma can be understood only in a social context.

It's My Life Now: Starting Over After an Abusive Relationship or Domestic Violence, Meg Kennedy Dugan and Roger R. Hock, 2nd Edition, 2006. Domestic violence survivors know that leaving is not the end of the nightmare—it is the beginning of an often difficult and challenging journey toward healing and happiness. The book offers practical guidance, emotional reassurance, and psychological awareness needed to heal after leaving abusers.

Healing the Trauma of Domestic Violence: A Workbook for Women (New Harbinger Self-Help Workbook), Mari McCraig, MSW and Edward S/ Kubany, PhD, 2004. Many women who free themselves from violent domestic situations experience symptoms of post-traumatic stress disorder (PTSD) long after they achieve physical and emotional safety. If you've freed yourself from an abusive relationship but still suffer from its effects, these techniques can help you recognize the effects of trauma on your life and heal.

Changing Hurt to Hope

Each year, social service agencies across the country set aside October as Domestic Violence Awareness Month, a time to focus attention on an issue that far too often is kept unacknowledged and tacitly ignored. For YWCA Sonoma County, whose primary mission is to end domestic violence through awareness, education, and empowerment, October is the most important time for outreach activities.

In the late spring of 2010, a trio of volunteers met with then volunteer coordinator Donata Bohanec (now Mikulik) to brainstorm activities for the upcoming awareness month. Michelle Wing, a local author and poet, proposed the idea of a writers' series, putting out a call to the general community for submissions on the topic of domestic violence. The plan was fleshed out with the help of the other two volunteers, Stacy Carlese and Caryl Fuller, and given the name Changing Hurt to Hope: Writers Speak Out Against Domestic Violence.

That first year, the organizers had no idea if the plan would work. Were there actually writers who would respond to the call for submissions? Would people address this topic in poetry, short fiction, and memoir? If so, would they then be willing to come forward to read their words in a public venue?

Although the entries trickled in at first, they did arrive. By the September 15, 2010 deadline, twenty-two submissions had been received—enough to fill slots for three nights of readings in the previously chosen cities of Santa Rosa, Sebastopol, and Cloverdale.

Over the next three years, the call for submissions went out, and works continued to come in. As expected, many of the submitters were survivors of domestic violence. A few were authors and poets, who had simply taken the call for submissions as a writing prompt. The final collection of prose and poetry accumulated by 2013, however, touched upon many more lives. Among them were: adults who wrote about being child witnesses to a parent's abuse; a man whose sister had been killed by her batterer; mothers who had adopted children taken from homes where there was domestic violence; a social worker, speaking about what she saw in her daily work; and a man responding to a newspaper article he had read about an incident in his community.

The organizers of Changing Hurt to Hope originally intended the project as a series of reading events to create awareness for the general public. It turned into something much more inclusive and far reaching than that. Without any planning, the contributors to Changing Hurt to Hope represented every facet of the community: women and men, gay and straight, Anglo, black, Latino, Arab-American, age thirteen to seventy-five, affluent to socio-economically disadvantaged. Domestic violence crosses all lines, and these writings bear out that fact.

Additionally, the act of writing served as catharsis for many of the writers. Some of them had never spoken of the abuse, let alone written it down. When these writers came to one of the Changing Hurt to Hope venues, stood up in front of a live audience, and read their words aloud, they spoke their lives, their truths. Often, there were tears—but incredible healing at the same time.

Domestic violence almost always happens in isolation. Yet another unexpected result of this program was that these survivors, families, and loved ones of survivors, met one another. They sat in the same room together, and heard each other's stories. They embraced, they cried, they clapped, sometimes they cheered.

With the continuing support of YWCA, Michelle Wing has shepherded this program through four successful years, and is now entering the fifth anniversary season in 2014. Changing Hurt to Hope has expanded to include four cities with the addition of Sonoma. In 2013, the call for submissions went far and wide, thanks to a few blog posts. That year's program included a multi-media aspect for the first time, with a filmmaker, songwriters, and poets, and works coming from as far away as Georgia, Kansas, New Jersey, and Michigan.

Through this five-year journey, each writer has taken her or his own path. Some have visited just once. Some have become regular contributors. Some have used Changing Hurt to Hope as a way to tell their story of past abuse to a current spouse or family member. Some have written a story from long ago, cracking themselves open, then returned two or three years later, to tell a new tale, about how they have changed since that revelation. Some, after that moment of courage, reading their words, have gone on to advocacy work, helping other survivors of abuse. And the audiences, too, have been deeply affected, stirred by the resilience and the honesty of these women and men.

Many lives have been changed by the words on these pages. May one of them be yours.

About the Editors

Michelle Wing

Michelle Wing (MA, International Studies, University of Washington) is a poet and writer of creative nonfiction. She founded Changing Hurt to Hope: Writers Speak Out Against Domestic Violence in 2010, working as a volunteer with the YWCA Sonoma County, and continues to coordinate this annual reading series. As a survivor, she knows the importance of writing from her own healing journey. Her first volume of poetry, *Body on the Wall*, was released in May 2014. Two of her poems were shown in October 2012 at the California Museum in Sacramento at a special exhibit, *Creating Freedom: Art & Poetry of Domestic Violence Survivors.* Her piece, "Dreamwork," received first place honors. She has a fifteen-year background in community journalism, and writes a monthly literary column, *Off the Page*, which can be found online at www.sonomawest.com. Michelle is a board member and serves as the public relations director for Redwood Writers, the largest branch of the California Writers Club, and also serves as a board member for the Healdsburg Literary Guild. She blogs and posts her poetry at http://michellewing.com.

Ann Hutchinson

Ann Hutchinson's personal narratives and short works of fiction have been published in magazines and anthologies for nearly ten years, mostly as Ann Wilkes. Her first short memoir, about finding her sister, was published three times in various media. Ann is also a freelance writer, editor, and journalist. A currently active member of Redwood Writers, the local branch of the California Writers Club, Ann has also served on the board, and founded and coordinated a reading series that the club still offers. She has founded and coordinated various local critique groups and is an active member of Broad Universe, an international organization dedicated to promoting and serving women authors of speculative fiction. A survivor herself, Ann participated in Hurt to Hope two of the last four years. Struck by the anguish and the courage poured out in the stories and true accounts she heard at the readings, she determined they needed a broader audience. She approached Kate Farrell, who had experience publishing a similar anthology project, and together they contacted Michelle Wing, who had expressed a desire over the years to do such a venture, but had lacked the time and resources.

Kate Farrell

Kate Farrell (MLS, UC Berkeley), storyteller, author, and educator, taught language arts in high schools, colleges, and universities; founded the Word Weaving storytelling project in collaboration with the California Department of Education with a grant from the Zellerbach Family Fund; and published numerous educational materials. She was the founding editor for a series of anthologies, *Vintage Voices*, for Redwood Writers (2006-11); edited the anthology, *Wisdom Has a Voice: Every Daughter's Memories of Mother* (2011); and co-edited *Times They Were A-Changing: Women Remember the '60s &'70s* (2013)—Finalist, 2013 *Foreword Reviews* Book of the Year Award and Finalist, 2014 Indie Excellence Award. Kate is Membership Chair of Women's National Book Association and President of its San Francisco Chapter, board member of California Writers Club, Redwood Branch, and member, Story Circle Network.

About the Authors

Robyn Anderson
Losing Abby

Robyn Anderson and her long-term partner, Carolyn, adopted two girls (age four and six) from foster care. The elder, now twenty-one, was in residential treatment for a number of years with auditory and visual hallucinations caused by early childhood trauma. After graduating from the program, she chose to seek her birth father, a Crow Indian living on the Crow Reservation in Montana. It was not the reunion she imagined. She opted to stay in Montana, but not on the reservation. The younger girl, nineteen, successfully graduated from her own treatment program, but hung out with the "wrong" crowd. She returned home after treatment, but didn't stay. Her current whereabouts are unknown.

Dani Burlison
Loose Change

Dani Burlison has been a staff writer for a Bay Area alt-weekly, a columnist for *McSweeney's Internet Tendency,* and a book reviewer for *The Los Angeles Review.* Her writing appears in the *Chicago Tribune, The Rumpus, Utne Reader, Ploughshares Literary Magazine, Hip Mama Magazine, Shareable, Rad Dad Zine, Spirituality & Health Magazine, Chevy Culture Magazine, Prick of the Spindle,* and others. She is an alumna of the Squaw Valley Community of Writers, Lit Camp, and the Mendocino Coast Writers Conference. She has upcoming work in various online and print publications and a handful of anthologies. Her collection of essays was published in December 2013 and she is currently working on her second book.

Joshua Byrd
I Want Out

Joshua Byrd was born and raised in Atlanta, Georgia. His childhood experiences with poverty and violence stimulated his interest in restoring his childhood community and serving his country. He served eight years in the U. S. Marine Corps, worked as a sheriff's deputy, and graduated with top honors from several leadership institutes before going to law school. Joshua currently works as a business and political consultant, and he continues to write poetry and does spoken word poetry performances. His website is www.byrdspiration.com.

Ann Carranza
Domestic Violence in Three Poems

Writer Ann Carranza is a freelance correspondent with the Healdsburg Towns section of the *Press Democrat*. She lives with her husband of nearly thirty years, Leonel, and two rescue dogs— Chica, an obsessive Border collie, and Yoda, an imp of a Chihuahua. When she's not writing, you can find her, camera in hand, chasing creatures that flit, fly and crawl.

Sher Christian
Hope

The author of *Star Kissed Shadows, Divining Poetry,* and *Sweet Tongue: Assorted Poetry and Music,* Sher hosts the Third Sunday Poetry Reading in Sebastopol. John Christian accompanies Sher with keyboard music. Sher and John provide voice-over and music for audio projects. lusciouspoetry.typepad.com

Spirette Dotter
He's Not Abusive, Unlost & Unforgotten,
Fight-or-Flight Impaired

Spirette Dotter is a mom, grandma, poet, writer, fine artist, web designer, singer, and survivor. With an extraordinary history, she raised her six children and built an estate while single. She's passionate about her creative projects and non-profit work against domestic violence and the family court crisis.

Kate Farrell
Rebecca's Slippers

*See **About the Editors** for biographical information.*

Vilma Ginzberg
Ask Any Woman, Where the Scar Is

Vilma Ginzberg is a retired psychotherapist (1961-1996) and YWCA women's shelter board member from Wisconsin. She hosts Healdsburg Literary Guild's monthly Third Sunday Salon. Vilma has authored five books of poems: *Colors of Glass*, 2004, *Murmurs & Outcries*, 2007, *Snake Pit*, 2010, *I Don't Know How to Do This: Poems on Aging*, 2011, and *making noise*, 2013, and co-edited *Present at the Creation*, 2006. She also completed the first of three volumes of her memoir, *When the Iris Blooms*, in 2012. Vilma served as Healdsburg's Literary Laureate in 2008-2009.

Dianna L. Grayer
Fear to Fierceness, Thank You, Mama!

Dianna L. Grayer, Ph.D., is a marriage and family therapist in Petaluma and a core faculty member at Meridian University. She has published six children's books, a self-esteem workbook and CD, created her own workshop, "Stepping Into Fierceness," and shares her spoken word pieces at events that empower women to rise up. She loves being at the ocean to be gifted ideas to help in her work of inspiring people to show up authentically in their lives. She lives with her life partner, Sheridan Gold, and their animals.

Christy Hoss
Blood & Fire

Christy Hoss is a credentialed art teacher, writer, and inspirational speaker. Married to Kevin for twenty-five years, she has three teenage children and a houseful of fur-kids. Her painting, *The Tree of Life*, portraying freedom from the negative influences of domestic violence, was displayed as part of the *Creating Freedom* exhibit at the California Museum in Sacramento in the fall of 2012. She has been published recently in *Guideposts*, *Angels on Earth* magazine, and *Focus on the Family's ClubHouse* magazines.

Ann Hutchinson
Strangled, My Body Remembered

*See **About the Editors** for biographical information.*

Barbara Kephart Immel
Fragments

Barbara Kephart Immel is a graduate of the University of California, Santa Barbara, and the Stanford Professional Publishing Course. She lives in Sonoma County with her husband, son, and daughter. Her morning ritual is to make a cup of hot cocoa and coax her cat onto her lap before writing.

Megan Ingrassia
In the Darkest Times

Megan Ingrassia is a social worker dedicated to bettering the lives of older adults in her community. She is also an artist and full-time single mother of two teen-age boys. She has a background in decorative painting, has taught art to children, and led art therapy groups for Alzheimer's and stroke patients. In 2011, she acquired her Master's degree in Depth Psychology, her thesis work emphasizing the use of art as a tool for self-healing.

Diane Madrigal
A Woman in Search of God, I Am Not Dead

Diane Madrigal is a motivational speaker and creative writer. She has worked with women, children, and families in crisis for more than twenty-five years. She has written and directed several original scripts for women's ministry and is soon to publish her book, *Seasons of Healing.*

Ana Manwaring
Battered

Ana Manwaring writes for the *Petaluma Post*, teaches creative writing through Napa Valley College and is an editor at JAM Manuscript Consulting. She is the treasurer for Sisters in Crime NorCal and is active in Redwood and Napa Valley Writers. Watch for Ana's thriller, *The Hydra Effect*. You can visit her online at www.anamanwaring.com and anaelectures.word press.com.

Juanita J. Martin
No Rights, Fractured

Juanita J. Martin, Fairfield's first poet laureate, 2010-2012, is an award-winning poet, a freelance writer, and a performance artist. She is the author of *The Lighthouse Beckons,* a poetry collection. Her poems appear in *Blue Collar Review, SoMa Literary Review, Rattlesnake Review,* and *Bay Area Poets Review*. Her poem, "Emancipate Me," was accepted in the Benicia Historical Museum's exhibit *Freedom Is a Hard Bought Thing,* commemorating the 150th anniversary of the Emancipation Proclamation. She is active in the Ina Coolbrith Circle, Redwood Writers, Marin Poetry Center, and Benicia First Tuesday Poets. Juanita is working on a new book of poetry called *Quiet Intensity.* www.jmartinpoetwriter.com

Kalia Mussetter
Bearing Witness

Artist and writer Kalia Mussetter has written poems since she was little. Because poetry is art made with words, it has always allowed her to express things she otherwise couldn't. Secret violence plagued her outwardly successful family, so discovering this way to vent was extremely important.

Carrie Nassif
Carrying On

Carrie Nassif is a poet psychologist from the rural Midwest: wife of a woman, mother of two, daughter of none. She is a therapist and writing is her therapy. She says she is a "survivor, thriver and soul diver. Just like you." She is published in the *Pomona Valley Review 8* and the 2012 anthology *Off Channel*. For more of her writing, thoughts, and photography, go to monstersofourowndestiny. wordpress.com.

Madeleine Keegan O'Connell
Familiar Click

Madeleine Keegan O'Connell is the chief executive officer of YWCA Sonoma County—the leading provider of domestic violence services in our community. She is a fourth generation Sonoma County resident, dedicated to raising awareness of domestic violence in order to realize her organization's mission to end it. A first-time contributor to the Changing Hurt to Hope reading series, Madeleine is a student of the written word and enjoys creative writing and poetry.

Renelaine Pfister
Tainted Vows

Renelaine Pfister's non-fiction articles and poems have been published in the Philippines, including the national paper, *The Philippine Daily Inquirer*. She wrote a column for a newspaper in New Jersey from 2006-2008. Her flash fiction, *Crab*, was published in *Vintage Voices 2012* by Redwood Writers. Sonoma County watercolor artist, Sally Baker, chose her short story, "Cherries for Bidu," to accompany one of her paintings. Another story won a competition hosted by *Newbie Writers*. Her story, "Education by Ate Flora" is being published in an anthology.

Zara Raab
Victim Witness

Zara Raab, who now lives in Berkeley, raised a family in Sonoma County and lived there more than twenty years. She grew up on the North Coast, where her great-great-grandparents farmed, raised cattle and harvested tan oak. Her parents attended one-room schools. Her poems appear in *River Styx, Crab Orchard Re-*

view, Evansville Review, The Dark Horse, Arts & Letters, and elsewhere.

Peggy Raggio
Hidden Wounds

Peggy Raggio is the author of many poems, plays, and newspaper stories, telling of her travels from her birth in Atlanta, Georgia, in 1926, to life in California. She's also written of experiences in Poland in the 1990s, as a Peace Corps Volunteer, teaching ESL to college students, and her family genealogy. She lives with her piano, computer, and memories, in a beautiful senior apartment complex and enjoys her four children, thirteen grandkids and fifteen great grandchildren.

Margaret Raymond
Flight

Margaret Raymond is a former journalist, magazine editor, and broadcaster. At retirement she turned to fiction (nineteen novels, seven more under contract), melodramas (five produced), and poetry. She lives in Northern California with Fred, her pet ficus tree.

Lilith Rogers
Sometimes It Sneaks Up On You

Lilith Rogers is a long-time writer; gardener; environmentalist; lefty, lesbian feminist; mother; and grandmother, who has happily lived in Sonoma County for almost thirty years. She has recently self-published several children's picture books about a young deer with two moms and a book of poetry. Lilith is also the star of *Rachel Carson Returns,* a one-woman performance she created. Contact her at rachelcarsonreturns@gmail.com.

David Rosas
Eating in Silence

David Rosas is a Sonoma County native and a graduate of Santa Rosa Junior College and Sonoma State University. He has been published in the *Press Democrat* and a national Hispanic magazine. David is active in the Southwest section of Santa Rosa, and he is on the Roseland School Board and Santa Rosa Community Health Center Board. Hobbies include cooking, cycling, running, writing short stories, community murals, and remodeling bathrooms and kitchens.

Meta Strauss
Cinderella Tale

Meta Strauss began writing after moving to Sonoma in 2005 from her lifelong home, Houston, Texas. She is a member of Sonoma Writers Alliance, reads her work at Readers' Book Store's Random Acts and has had several short stories published in the *Sonoma Sun*. A novel, *Salvaging El Chico*, centered in a small west Texas town, will be released this fall. She is a former CASA (Child Advocates) volunteer and has a passionate interest in eradicating domestic abuse.

Jaz Sufi
An Open Letter to Rihanna from Lilith

Bay Area native Jaz Sufi is a poet and excavator of the human condition. At eighteen, she became the slammaster of the legendary Santa Cruz Indie Slam and the youngest slammaster of a Poetry Slam, Inc. (PSI)-certified venue in the country. Later that year, she assistant-coached her team to place eighth in the 2011 National Poetry Slam.

Deborah Taylor-French
An Unfathomable Truth

Deborah Taylor-French writes mystery, poetry, and nonfiction. A columnist for the *Sonoma County Gazette*, she writes *Cotati…Heart*

& *Soul.* She also blogs for dog lovers and animal welfare at dogleadermysteries.com and "Be the Change for Animals." Her top passions are reading and writing myth, mystery, and metamorphosis. Deborah nurtures writers through Redwood Writers, a branch of the California Writers Club, as author support group facilitator. A former guest artist for California's Artists in the Schools, Deborah holds a Masters in Dance Education from UCLA. Having raised five adopted dogs, two rabbits, and one adored, adopted daughter, she lives with her husband and one adopted house rabbit, Tokyo Tuxedo.

Ed Thompson
How Far Have We Fallen?

Ed Thompson, born in 1937, has lived in Sonoma County for twenty-four years. He has a master's degree in English, and taught high school English and history for forty-one years. He retired in 2004, and continues to write and direct plays for a high school drama group.

Erin Treanor
The Hardest Part

Erin Treanor is an actress, producer, director, and stage manager in the theater scene in the L.A. area, and is currently working as a casting director for TV. She is madly, passionately in love with the theater. Her childlike refusal to face reality has only ignited the fire of creativity that burns brilliance into everything it touches. Playwriting is no exception. Erin is thrilled to be involved in such an important project. She would like to thank her family for their constant love and support.

Janet Vallance
House of Mirrors, Night After Court, This Heart

Primarily a massage therapist and herbalist, Janet Vallance has been writing poetry for 30 years. She is inspired by the poetry of Lucille Clifton, Alice Walker, Anne Sexton, and Marge Piercy. She has two awesome, grown children and loves swimming holes.

Juliana Marie Van Guilder
My World Tipped Over

Juliana Marie Van Guilder, thirteen, is an eighth grader in Santa Rosa. She loves sports and enjoys helping others. She has served in Women to Women ministries and special events, hosting, directing, as well as participating, in several original scripts since age five. She loves photography and her dog, Elvis the Hound dog.

Angela Monique Webb-Pigg
Think, Speak, Love

Angela Monique Webb-Pigg is a twenty-four-year-old Santa Rosa native. She is a Santa Rosa Junior College graduate, and intent on finishing her Bachelor of Arts in theater/writing. Angela has kept a private journal since the age of thirteen and has experimented with poetry the last few years. Growing up in a home filled with hurt and abuse, Angela found writing served as a priceless aid through her journey to mend her fears and keep hope alive in her life.

Kitty Wells
After the Violence—Haiku

Kitty Wells has worked in the areas of domestic violence and child abuse since 1984 and has been a Marriage and Family Therapist for more than twenty-five years. A cherished part of her work is with trauma survivors, using talk, art, and play therapies, EFT, EMDR, ho'oponopono, and hypnosis.

Leonore Wilson
The Cage, That Easter

Leonore Wilson is the mother of three sons in their early twenties. Her husband is a scientist. She lives in the wilds of Northern California. Like it or not, she comes from generations of rugged females keeping nature both fertile and sacred. She has won awards as well as fellowships for her work and has published in *Poets Against the War, Madison Review, Sing Heavenly Muse, Rattle, Quarterly*

West, *Third Coast*, *Pedestal*, *Laurel Review*, *Pif*, *DMQ Review*, and *Unlikely Stories*. She is on the MFA and River of Words boards at St. Mary's College.

Michelle Wing
Gifts, Body on the Wall, How I Became a Poet,
Even a Woman, Driving Free

*See **About the Editors** for biographical information.*

Farrell Winter
The Knife

Farrell Winter has written and edited short stories, magazine articles, film reviews, and scripts and storyboards for community-access cable television. He is currently working on publishing his first novel and researching his autobiography. He is a member of the Redwood Branch of the California Writers Club and of the Bay Area Independent Publishers Association. He lives in Santa Rosa, California, with his family, and may be contacted at zalmoxis@sbcglobal.net.

Louise Young
Tippy's Tale

Louise is a former public school teacher who worked with many students who lived with violence at home. She hopes that as awareness grows of the damage children suffer from violence of all kinds, adults will learn to respect a child's need for stability and harmony at home and at school.

Made in the USA
Charleston, SC
04 September 2014